THE KINSMAN'S CODE:

THE MYSTERIES AND SECRETS OF HIS RETURN

By David Lindsey

Copyright © 2012 by David Lindsey

The Kinsman's Code: The Mysteries and Secrets of His Return
by David Lindsey

Printed in the United States of America

ISBN 9781622301775

All rights reserved solely by the author. The author guarantees all contents are original and do not infringe upon the legal rights of any other person or work. No part of this book may be reproduced in any form without the permission of the author. The views expressed in this book are not necessarily those of the publisher.

Unless otherwise indicated, Bible quotations are taken from the King James Bible, Key Study Edition. Copyright © 1979 by A.J. Holman Co.

www.xulonpress.com

THE KINSMAN'S CODE:
THE MYSTERIES AND SECRETS OF HIS RETURN
By David Lindsey

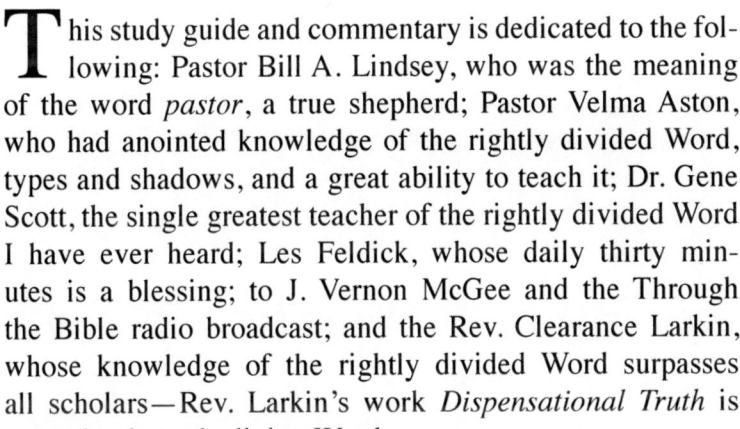

This study guide and commentary is dedicated to the following: Pastor Bill A. Lindsey, who was the meaning of the word *pastor*, a true shepherd; Pastor Velma Aston, who had anointed knowledge of the rightly divided Word, types and shadows, and a great ability to teach it; Dr. Gene Scott, the single greatest teacher of the rightly divided Word I have ever heard; Les Feldick, whose daily thirty minutes is a blessing; to J. Vernon McGee and the Through the Bible radio broadcast; and the Rev. Clearance Larkin, whose knowledge of the rightly divided Word surpasses all scholars—Rev. Larkin's work *Dispensational Truth* is second only to the living Word.

To my wife Stacy, who truly lives the life and has blessed me beyond all understanding; to my sons Shawn and Eric—they have made me a proud father; to my granddaughter Isabelle, the light of my life; to my mother, who has been a rock, a steady and loving influence in my life; to my mother-in-law, who has loved me as a son; to my brother Richard, who loves the Lord; and to Jimmy and Carolyn— thank you.

To friends: Robert and Kelly, Judy, Frank, Jim, Tom, Kelly, Nancy, Don, Bill, Rick, Gary and Kris, Tom and Patty Billy, Marylou, Jimmy and Carolyn, Bob, Carol and Chuck, Artys and Ed, Cathy and George, Marvin, Lisa, Michael and Katy, Vince, Ronnie, Dick, Darren, Jonnie, Julie, Ann, Keith, Lorna, Wanda, Norma, Nancy, Reba, Lila, and Judy

That which is last is first.

To the Son, the Lord Jesus Christ, "the Bright and Morning Star," first and foremost—His glory is above all, for it pleased the Father to give all things unto Him, of Him, and secure in Him, and by whose "stripes I am healed and by His shed blood I am saved."

To God the Father, first and foremost, for His eternal plan of salvation. Through His love, grace, and mercy and by His power and glory He hath revealed it to His sheep.

To the Holy Ghost for giving me revelation of the Lord Jesus Christ, for His teaching and leading me to the right pastors, teachers, and authors.

To God be the glory forever and ever. Amen.

FOREWORD

To understand what time it is in Almighty God's plan and purpose for the ages, we must understand where we are within the plan and how we got here. We must start at the beginning and uncover the code to the secrets and mysteries of the ages which will enable us to understand the ending, for He is both the beginning and the ending. This study will contain commentary by the author based on the Word of God. Every attempt is made to keep all commentary based on sound doctrine from the living Word of God, not holding to any one or more denominations, but by the Holy Ghost.

This study is intended to be a journey and revelation of God's Word, for the edifying of the saints and to offer sound information to those who wish to be among the saints, saved by the finished works of Jesus Christ. We will review a wide range of topics and uncover the mysteries and secrets of the Almighty. We will cover a vast time period and use the codes and language of God to reach the conclusions concerning the issues of our past, our present, and our future. We will unlock the salvation code, for salvation is where the believer's journey begins.

This book is provided to help believers and those who seek understanding to realize how God has provided the road to salvation by His Son Jesus Christ and His finished work. It will reveal how He discloses to us through codes and mathematics the answers to mysteries and secrets of His Word. Grace, a free gift from God, is the power unto salvation, and He has made these secrets and mysteries known to us in these last days.

Are we able and is there a requirement for us to add something to His work? Is His work perfect? Is our salvation completely or conditionally given? Must we work to keep it? And, once obtained, can it be lost? If we've been given the gift would He take it back? Are we in fact close to the edge? Is the rapture real, and if so when will it happen? Is Jesus returning? Did Jesus claim to be God and is He God? What is the order of things yet to come? Is there work left for Him to do? If so how much work is left for Him to do?

These questions are at the top of the list. Let us see and hear what the living Word says about grace by faith: how, why, and where this grace comes from; why, how, and by whom it is brought to us; and by whom it is kept. Where are we and our world headed, and how are we going to get there? Does anybody really know what time it is? Is it soon to end, and how does it end? Is God through with Israel?

The codes and language of God are not regularly taught in our churches today and certainly not taught and understood by the TV evangelists of our day; the only math they understand is how much money they can obtain. We will unlock *The Kinsman's Code* concerning our salvation through the finished works of Jesus Christ and see the truth and answers to many questions

As I See It...

Jesus Christ is the Son of God, a part of the Elohim triune God: Father, Son, and Holy Ghost. I believe that He struck a tent of human flesh and came to earth born of a virgin. Jesus our Savior fulfills all law required for a kinsman-redeemer.

He offered the kingdom to Israel and was rejected. He died on the cross, was buried, rose from the dead, and is alive. He was seen by many witnesses and now sits at the right hand of the Father making intercession on behalf of all who have received Him by faith.

I believe that He paid the sin debt for all who believe and that we are saved by grace through our faith in the finished works of His life, death, and resurrection. He has fulfilled and will fulfill all Scripture. I also believe He will return in the clouds to call out His Church, which is both His Body and His Bride if you will. After seven years He will return from on high and touch the earth, save Israel, and rule and reign for one thousand years. He will rebuild heaven and earth and eternity will begin.

The Guide

Within this study and commentary we will use capital letters for all divine pronouns (He, Him, His, and Himself). We will look at many of the names our Lord has used within the living Word, such as Son of God, Ancient of Days, Kinsman-Redeemer, Bright and Morning Star, etc. We will also use capital letters when referring to the Church, the Body and the Bride. This is done to distinguish and identify Him and what belongs to Him. It will aid us in unlocking the secrets and mysteries of the Almighty. It will help us reveal the code and language He uses to speak to His people. No Scripture is misquoted, no Scripture is altered. Capital letters are used to provide insight and clarity.

He is the first and the last, the centerpiece of all history. He is the Head of the Church, He is the Bridegroom, and He is the Firstborn. He is also to be the Lord of Lords and the King of Kings, and all knees will bow and all tongues confess that Jesus Christ is Lord.

I believe that the Bible is the living Word of God! All Scripture will be quoted using the King James Bible. We will start at the beginning and go to the end; we will see through this process what the Word says of our past, our present, and our future by rightly dividing the Word of truth.

We will begin with five secrets of Scripture and the living Word; we will take a hard look at to whom the Word speaks, and why the Word speaks to different classes of people. We will review the dividing of the Word, the ages and dispensations of the Word, and how science and the Word are in fact in complete harmony. We will review the covenants and with whom they are made. We will look at the mathematics of God and why He speaks through numbers. We will question old theories of archeology and modern science. We will establish types and shadows and why they are so important to His Word. We will look deeply at the mystery and use of parables and why He was and is speaking to us through the use of parables. We shall uncover secrets and mysteries that God has kept hidden in Himself until His appointed time.

We will examine our Lord, our Kinsman-Redeemer, the Bright and Morning Star, the Creator, the Passover Lamb, and the Prince of Peace. We will examine the purpose of the cross, the purpose of the shed blood and His glorious resurrection. We will ask the questions of eternal security, of works, of faith, and of grace. We will look at the need for future work: how, why, and when will it be finished? We will review our findings, reach conclusions, and hopefully expand our faith and obtain rest.

We will visit the modernist doctrines and teachings of the day based on the Word of God and what it says on the topics of this movement. We will pursue false doctrines and teachings, but will slander no one by name or any denomination by name. We will unlock the code and reveal mysteries and secrets of the rightly divided Word of truth. We will be workmen found worthy. Let's begin.

CHAPTER 1: FIVE SECRETS OF SCRIPTURE:
CODE NAME THE WORD 19

    A. Secret One: Things Are Settled 19
    B. Secret Two: How He Views It................................20
    C. Secret Three: It Is Not Private...................................20
    D. Secret Four: Not the Natural Man.........................21
    E. Secret Five: For His Name's Sake 21
    F. The Word of God 22

CHAPTER 2: RIGHTLY DIVIDE THE WORD:
CODE NAME TRUTH..25

    A. The Jew 26
    B. The Gentile..27
    C. The Church...29
    D. The Law 32
    E. Grace 34
    F. Faith 36
    G. Sin 39
    H. Salvation 42
    I. Atonement..49
    J. Redemption 50

CHAPTER 3: THE THIRTEEN-NUMBERED CLOCK:
CODE NAME FIRST AND LAST 54

    A. The Five Ages 55
    B. The Eight Dispensations 69

CHAPTER 4: SCIENCE AND THE BIBLE:
CODE NAME CREATOR 87

    A. Creation: The Earthly Code 87
    B. Creation: The Heavenly Code 90

CHAPTER 5: THE ISRAEL AGREEMENT:
CODE NAME COVENANT 94

    A. The Covenant with Noah 94
    B. The Covenant with Abraham 95
    C. The Covenant with Moses 97
    D. The Covenant with David 98
    E. The Covenant with Reborn Israel 99

CHAPTER 6: THE SECRET LANGUAGE OF GOD:
CODE NAME MATHEMATICS 101

    A. Mathematics: The Code 101
    B. Mathematics: The Language 103
    C. Mathematics: The Ancient Witness....................109

CHAPTER 7: SECRETS OF THE FUTURE:
CODE NAME TYPES AND SHADOWS 117

    A. Types and Shadows of Jesus Christ 118
    B. Types and Shadows of the Cross 121
    C. Types and Shadows of Israel...............................122

CHAPTER 8: MYSTERIES OF HEAVEN: CODE NAME PARABLES 126

    A. New Cloth on Old Garments 129
    B. New Wine in Old Bottles 129
    C. The Hidden Treasure 130
    D. The Pearl of Great Price 130
    E. The Net 132
    F. The Two Debtors 133
    G. The Lost Coin 134
    H. The Pharisee and the Publican 134

CHAPTER 9: MYSTERIES OF GOD: CODE NAME PAUL'S GOSPEL 138

    A. The Gospel of the Blood 140
    B. The Gospel of the Cross 143
    C. The Gospel of Grace by Faith 144
    D. The Gospel of the Resurrection 146
    E. The Mystery of the Church 149
    F. The Gospel of Judgment 151

CHAPTER 10: JESUS: CODE NAME KINSMAN-REDEEMER 154

    A. The Alpha and Omega 154
    B. The Broken Body 155
    C. The Blood of the Lamb 156
    D. The Resurrection 158

CHAPTER 11: THE SALVATION CODE: 53787 161

    A. No Other Name 161
    B. Not by Works of the Flesh 163
    C. The Just Shall Live by Faith 167

CHAPTER 12: THE COMING OF THE KING: CODE NAME MIGHTY GOD 171

    A. The Future Work 172

CHAPTER 13: THERE IS NONE LIKE ME: CODE NAME ALPHA 185

    A. There Can Be Only One: Code Name I AM 185
    B. Does Anybody Really Know What Time It Is? ... 189

CHAPTER 14: IN THESE LAST DAYS: CODE NAME OMEGA 194

    A. Are We Before or After? Code Name the Cross ... 194
    B. Jesus Christ: Code Name the Only Name 196

AUTHOR'S INTRODUCTION

There have been influences in my life and that is clear and easy to see for any student of the rightly divided Word. All commentary will be based solely upon the Word and what the Scriptures say to us. Allowing the Holy Ghost to speak is difficult for the natural man. However when we pray for Him to speak He does; it is sometimes easy to hear Him and yet hard for us to understand Him. We must allow our spirit to work; for the Word is said to be sweet to the taste but bitter to the belly.

There is no attempt to tell anyone what church they should attend, only that when we attend we should take what we hear and then look to the Word. There are no dates set pertaining to those things which are surely soon to come. While there is considerable information located in this study pertaining to end times, it is not the focal point of the work.

This study is designed to allow us to see for ourselves that we are a created people, on a created planet residing in a created universe, managed and controlled by a mighty God. We want to see that the Word of God is a living Word. That the sin debt has been paid, and as such we have been granted rightness with God the Father. We have been bought with a price; in fact we are both a hidden treasure and a pearl of great price. Through the Son of God, Jesus Christ, we have been bought and paid for by His precious blood. We want to unlock the code and the language of the Ancient of Days and uncover the truth of His eternal plan for the ages.

This author has reached certain conclusions based on the living Word. These are conclusions concerning the sin debt, God coming in the flesh, and the requirements for salvation and resurrection. Conclusions have been made concerning the many conflicts that are coming to the earth between now and His triumphant return. However I leave the final conclusions to each reader.

The Word of God is a living Word. It will show us both history past and history present, and both with 100 percent perfection. This author has concluded that it can be counted on to correctly foretell the future of history as it has the past and present.

We must look within the Word at whom history relates to as well as to whom it is directed, and the subject of the history. The living Word (rightly divided) shows the power, the authority, the majesty, the love, and the grace of God. It shows His compassion, mercy, and justice. Through it all it clearly shows His relationship with the Jews, the Gentiles, and His Church and how these three groups are all judged on a different application of the rules all stemming from the same rule. We will examine where we are located at a certain point in His future history and discover that which is to come and how it will affect us depending on which group we belong to.

While the Church is both typed and shadowed in the Old Testament, the Church is not located and did not exist in the Old Testament. So the Old Testament is related to the Jew and Gentile. The New Testament consists of both Jewish books and letters, directed primarily to the Jew and the Church, as well as to the natural man and the spiritual man.

The letters of the apostle Paul relate to the Church. The Pauline epistles are Church doctrine. The Church is made up of a people out of many nations, denominations, and tongues. The Gospels are directed to the Jew and concern Jesus' coming to His people, the nation of Israel. The letters of John, Peter, Jude, and James were written to convert Jews who would become members of the Church. It was Paul and Paul alone whom Christ sent to the Gentiles. There is very little directed to Gentile nations; however as we will see that which is said is important.

All Scripture is the Word of God, and as a result all Scripture is for reproof, understanding, and knowledge. What we want to understand is: to whom the Word is speaking, what the subject is, and the context of what we are reading.

For example James opens his letter "to the twelve tribes that are scattered abroad." While he is addressing both believers and would-be believers, they are all Jewish. The Church is not nor ever has been referred to as the twelve tribes. Therefore while James writes one of the most powerful statements of faith, and it is for our knowledge, it is not written to the Church but rather to Jews who were believers.

The letter of James is estimated to have been written before the first Council of Jerusalem, around 42 AD to 45 AD, about the time Paul was working on his first mission. According to Acts, at this time Gentiles were not yet accepted in the temples, and the Jews had very little if any contact with Gentiles; it was not lawful. The first 40 percent of the book of Acts clearly states this fact. Through Paul, by Jesus Christ, would come the mysteries and secrets of the Church, the Body and the Bride. The gospel of Paul would both reveal and clarify the hidden things of God.

We do not take that which is directed to the Jew and apply it to the Church. Likewise we do not apply what is directed to the Church to the Jew. We apply neither to the Gentile, nor the Gentile to either. Gentiles are Gentiles, Jews are Jews, and the Church—the Body and the Bride—are both.

Let us look at it this way: the creation is to all people, Jew and Gentile, the law to the nation of Israel, the Jew. The grace of God is to the Church. Past history is past, current history is current, and future history is still future. To unlock these secrets we must rightly divide the Word.

This author makes no attempt to pass judgment upon anyone, by name or denomination, but rather state facts, and if the shoe should fit wear it if you will. As we will see from the Word there is but one narrow way to salvation. However narrow it may be, it is wide enough to be offered to all. It is completely free and comes with a full 100 percent lifetime guarantee. It is not about our works, it is about His works. It is not about us being little gods, it is about Him being God, and there is none other. It is not about our glory, it is about His glory, and there is none like Him.

I personally am not capable of seeing the Father unless as a free gift through the Son, Jesus Christ. He is my only hope. I know who and what I am, weak, but He is strong. He is my Kinsman-Redeemer; He has purchased me by His blood. Those who have been called know the Shepherd's voice and He speaks of grace, mercy, love, salvation, and resurrection. This is what is said by the Word to the born-again believer.

CHAPTER ONE

FIVE SECRETS OF SCRIPTURE: CODE NAME THE WORD

Before we build our faith on the Solid Rock we want to establish the understanding of five secrets of truth by Scripture. These five truths will assist us in our study. It establishes how we should build our life and our faith in the Word of God. These five truths will underpin all that we will see in our study. They shall sit at the entrance to our house, that all should know.

Secret One: Things Are Settled

"For ever, O Lord, thy word is settled in heaven" (Psalm 119:89).

This should not be hard for us to understand. The Word of God and all that it says, reveals, and explains is settled in heaven. That which relates to the Father, Son, and Holy Ghost is in complete agreement. It has only that which it says. Not of man, church, or denomination. Rather the truth as revealed by the Holy Ghost to each writer of each book or letter. For we know that all were inspired by the Holy

Ghost. Therefore we know that God has settled the truth, purpose, and meaning of the living Word. We will see, hear, and understand that in these last days we have been spoken to by the Son of God.

Secret Two: How He Views It

"Thou shall be fuel for the fire: thy blood shall be in the midst of the land; thou shalt no more be remembered: for I the Lord have spoken it" (Ezekiel 21:32).

"...and calleth those things which be not as though they were" (Romans 4:17).

"The thing which hath been, it is that which shall be; and that which is done is that which shall be done: and there is no new thing under the sun" (Ecclesiastes 1:9).

Let us have understanding; God sees those things that are not as though they already were. When He speaks, it is done. It does not matter how long it takes to be completed; when He speaks it, it must happen. We can call it history written in advance.

Secret Three: It Is Not Private

"Knowing this first, that no prophecy of scripture is of any private interpretation" (2 Peter 1:20).

There are two important fundamentals here. First, be watchful of the preacher, teacher, priest, imam, and TV evangelist who teaches some new meaning from the Word, for there is nothing new under the sun. The true purpose of the Word is to reveal Almighty God in all His ways and show forth the truth and glory of Jesus Christ. Second, the

Word will always witness of itself, and the Holy Ghost will confirm the truth of what it says. Study not a scripture but the context and the subject matter as well, rightly dividing the Word of truth.

Secret Four: Not the Natural Man

"But the natural man receiveth not the things of the Sprit of God: for they are foolishness unto him: neither can he know them, because they are spiritually discerned" (1 Corinthians 2:14).

"For if a man think himself to be something, when he is nothing, he deceiveth himself" (Galatians 6:3).

Here we are being informed by the Word; the natural man simply cannot understand the things of God, therefore the natural man cannot receive the things of God. For if we cannot understand, how then would we receive? Yet day after day preachers preach and teachers teach not knowing what they preach or teach. They want to save the natural man. They try to remove a speck out of someone's eye while in their own eye is a beam. There are even those who make the foolish claim that they have overcome sin in the flesh. That's so sad for the Word is clear: the natural man receives not the things of God.

Secret Five: For His Name's Sake

"I write unto you, little children, because your sins are forgiven you for His name's sake" (1 John 2:12).

"Blotting out the handwriting of ordinances that was against us, which was contrary to us, and took it out of the way, nailing it to His cross" (Colossians 2:14).

Let us put this clearly into focus. We are to know and study as one who was, is, and forever shall be forgiven. Our forgiveness is provided by the finished works of the Lord Jesus Christ. He nailed the ordinances against us to His cross. Our sin is forgiven for His name's sake.

It is upon these five secrets of Scripture that we will build on the Solid Rock, to see and hear His mercy, grace, and love. We are to show ourselves approved, "a workman that need not be ashamed rightly dividing the word of truth."

The Word of God

The Word of God, the Bible, was written during a period of approximately sixteen hundred years, from 1492 BC to 100 AD. It was written by kings, judges, deliverers, fishermen, shepherds, tax collectors, great seers of God, a doctor, the educated, and a Roman citizen. There are sixty-six books and letters: thirty-nine Old Testament books and twenty-seven New Testament books and letters. The great book of Isaiah has sixty-six chapters and shows all mountain peaks of prophecy. It is the book the Lord read from when He first offered Israel the kingdom.

The Bible was written in the mountains, in the deserts, by the rivers, and in the courts of kings. It was written in the wilderness, in the temple, in bondage, in prison, and on the lonely Island of Patmos in solitude and exile. The common denominator is that all were instructed by the Holy Ghost, inspired and informed by the same.

The Bible is both a progressive and a transformational collection of books and letters. The judges knew more than the patriarchs, the prophets more than the judges, and the apostles more than the prophets. Within the book of Acts we transfer from the dispensation of law to the dispensation of grace by faith.

The Old Testament and New Testament cannot be separated; you cannot see the new without the old, for the new brings to life that which was foretold in the old. The Old Testament is not a collection of stories but rather a record of certain historical events relating to us certain truths that seem extremely important to Almighty God. In other words, what we have is what is important to the plan and purpose of Almighty God.

At the time of its writing, the Word reports that which was, that which is, and that which is to come. In its history it has become fulfillment, and that which is to be fulfilled. It is always history written in advance.

The scribes did not write in chapter and verse, they wrote books and letters, and the Word of God should be read as any other book or letter. It is when we take Scripture out of context that misunderstanding can result.

The Word contains three types of language: figurative, symbolic, and literal. In most cases we can see the figurative and symbolic language used by the context, or confirmed within the Scriptures. The rest should be taken as literal. It also speaks to us through the use of mathematics using these codes to confirm or highlight the text.

While the Bible is not intended to be a world history book, as mentioned, it does contain selected world history within itself. It is also not a science book, yet selected information concerning science is disclosed within its pages. Both in the areas of history and science we are given the information as God wants us to have it. He did not, nor does He intend to, discuss that which is important to Him with anyone. Who shall be His counsel? His counsel is of Himself.

The Word of God is written to three groups of people for their learning and understanding, not to people in general but rather in part to three different classes of people: the Jew, the Gentile, and the Church.

"Give none offence, neither to the Jews, nor to the Gentiles, nor to the church of God" (1 Corinthians 10:32).

This is a condensed study of the living Word of God. As has been said we make every attempt to base all commentary on Scripture. We will cover a wide range of subject matters and a vast amount of time. It is designed to help us reach a certain conclusion: that God created all things and all things have been given to Jesus Christ. That it is our faith in the risen Jesus Christ and His finished works which is the only power unto salvation. It is also designed to persuade each of us to open our Bibles, confirm, and study.

May the Sprit of God, the Holy Ghost, instruct us, teach us, and guide us to the blessings of His living Word. Amen.

CHAPTER TWO

RIGHTLY DIVIDE THE WORD: CODE NAME TRUTH

In this chapter we will review the three distinct people that the living Word speaks to and the time period that the Word is dealing with. We will look within the Word and begin to see how God deals with each of these three groups. We will present short, pointed views and Scripture to support our understanding. We will review the law and its purpose and to whom it was given. We will look at grace and how God provides this gift. We will examine the great importance God places on faith, and why.

We will look at sin in relation to why sin is and what sin is. We will spend time on redemption, salvation, and atonement and how they travel from the Old Testament, hidden in types and shadows, into the New Testament fulfillment. We will look at the two creations, the natural man and the spirit man. We will examine the three classes of people the Bible speaks to: the Jew, the Gentile, and the Church.

The Jew

For almost forty-two hundred years, under all forms of governments and civilizations, conditions of bondage and oppression, the Jewish people have maintained their own laws, beliefs, customs, and habits.

They are a most remarkable people; no other people can trace their lineage and history as far into the past as they are able to do. They created the first alphabet; they had literature before most nations had letters. Dispersed into all nations and cultures, they survived without a homeland for 2,555 years. They have watched as Assyria, Egypt, Babylon, the Medes and Persians, the Greeks, and the Romans all rose to great power and subsequently fell. During most of this time they were without a country and without a homeland.

Through the many trials and tribulations the Jewish people continue to prosper. Leading Jewish men and women have been at the forefront of history from Abraham to the apostle Paul right through till this day. In such fields as medicine, education, business, finance, and science the Jewish people have contributed to the world's advancement. They have made contributions in almost every field and part of our lives. They have won more Nobel prizes than any other race or group of people in world history.

From the nation of Assyria, to Egypt, Babylon, Media and Persia, Greece, and Rome, they have been constantly oppressed and looked down upon. They have gone in and out of slavery and have been killed and attacked more than all other nations or groups of people for over four thousand years! Why? For His name's sake, but they have survived.

In the past 150 years the Jews have endured the persecution of nations such as England, Spain, France, Russia, and Germany's Holocaust. Millions have been killed, starved, and tortured; billions of dollars in property, cash, land, and other assets have been stolen by these nations, yet still the Jews have pressed on.

During their history no nationality of people has had more blessings and more sorrow than the Jewish people. The history of God's dealing with the nation of Israel continues to unfold in both the Old Testament as well as the New Testament.

The Word of God is a living Word and is alive today. From the pages of our newspapers and all the cable news we can handle, we can read the events in the living Word of God, for when rightly divided it continues to be history written in advance.

On May 14, 1948, God brought back from the valley of dry bones a nation. On that date God caused the fig tree to bloom, and the nation of Israel was born again. Through 2555 years of dealing with His people God resurrected a nation from the dead (Exodus 37:11-28, John 24:32-34).

When Frederick the Great wanted one word for the Bible's inspiration his preacher replied, "The Jew."

History marches on to the time that is called the "time of Jacob's trouble."

The Gentile

Gentiles are all people who are not Jews. Therefore it is correct to include all nations as Gentile nations, and all people who are not Jewish are Gentiles.

When the Lord called Abraham all people could be considered Gentiles including Abraham. Abraham became the first Hebrew and Isaac the seed of this set-apart people. Almighty God granted unto Abraham land that was and is forever promised to the nation of Israel.

The royal land grant extends from the river of Egypt to the Euphrates from north of Damascus to Kadesh on the south (Genesis 15:18; Ezekiel 48:1-29).

Abraham's grandson Jacob has his name changed by God to Israel. Through him are born twelve sons, and they become the twelve tribes (Genesis 32:24-28).

After the death of Solomon the tribes are divided: ten become known as Israel and two, Benjamin and Judah, become Judah. In 721 BC Assyria carries the ten (Israel) into bondage and in 606 BC the other two (Judah) are taken into bondage by Babylon, and the time of the Gentiles begins.

Let us not confuse or combine the times of the Gentiles with the fullness of the Gentiles as the two represent two completely different things.

"And they shall fall by the edge of the sword, and shall be led away captive into all nations, and Jerusalem shall be trodden down by the Gentiles, until the times of the Gentiles be fulfilled" (Luke 21:24).

The time of the Gentiles as we can clearly see speaks of earthly kingdoms and certainly implies by the use of the word "time" that at some point God is going to again turn His heart toward His covenant people: Israel.

The fullness of the Gentiles refers to those who are called out by the testimony of the Holy Ghost. These are those who are gathered out of all nations, for His name, His Church, His Body, and His Bride.

"For I would not, brethren, that ye should be ignorant of this mystery, lest ye be wise in your own conceits, that blindness in part has happened to Israel, until the fullness of the Gentiles be brought in" (Romans 11:25).

We know both from history and Scripture that in 606 BC the time of the Gentiles began. It is here that a young Hebrew named Daniel who walks in righteousness before the Lord is carried into bondage to Babylon.

Nebuchadnezzar, the Babylonian king, has a disturbing dream, and the king's men of magic and his soothsayers cannot explain it. Daniel, through the revelation of the Holy Ghost, is shown both the dream and the understanding of the dream.

It consists of the coming Gentile nations that shall rise and fall and be against Israel. Beginning with the head of gold, arms and chest of silver, torso of brass, legs of iron, and feet of iron and clay, four of these have come on the scene and left, and one is yet to come. These kingdoms coincide with the beast kingdoms of both Daniel and Revelation.

Therefore we see that from 606 BC four of these kingdoms have in fact come and gone: Babylon, Media-Persia, Greece, and Rome. These kingdoms are described with such detail as to not mistake who they are. We can therefore assume the fifth will at some point in the near future also come, and seven years later it too will be gone. This will close the times of the Gentiles.

The Church

First let us review what the Church is not; it is not the continuation of the dispensation of the Jew. If the Word of God put Moses and the law in one dispensation and Christ and the Church in another then we should leave it as God intended it.

Let's look at some simple lessons, allowing the living Word to speak. When the cry came out of the wilderness by John the Baptist, his message was "the kingdom of heaven is at hand." The Lord sent out the Twelve and seventy to proclaim the same. Israel as a nation rejected their king; the establishing of that kingdom was postponed—it was not abandoned, but postponed. We should understand the parable of the "nobleman farmer" who has traveled to a far country to receive a kingdom and returns (Luke 19:11-27).

The Church should never be confused with the kingdom; it is never called a kingdom. It is identified as a House (1 Timothy 3:14), a Temple (1 Corinthians 3:16-17), a Body (1 Corinthians 12:27-31), and a Bride (Ephesians 5:23-32). Therefore it is clear that the Church is not the kingdom spoken of by the prophets or in the Gospels. The kingdom that was at hand was not a mystery; it was and is well known and never has been a mystery.

On the other hand the Church is a mystery, given to Paul and to Paul alone (Ephesians 3:1-11). That it is still a mystery can be seen in both the many false religions and doctrines of the day. Here we can see that Paul is naming the dispensation of grace, that the Church is a mystery, that it is by eternal purpose, and that the Gentiles would become joint-heirs with the Jews in this new thing, the Church.

We know by Paul's message to the Romans that the Gentile being saved was not the mystery (Romans 9:24-30) but rather the forming of a new thing, combining both Jew and Gentile, called the Church—that was the mystery.

In Acts 15:13-18 we see that we are a people called for His name, and thus this dispensation is not to convert the world but rather to gather a people to be called out of the world.

In Ephesians 1:22-23 we see Jesus as the Head and the Church as the Body.

In Ephesians 4:4-6 we see one body (Church), one spirit (Holy Ghost), one Lord (Jesus), one faith, one baptism (of the Holy Ghost), and one God and Father of all and above all.

Many people misunderstand the purpose of this dispensation. Again it is not to save society but rather individuals out of society who comprise His Body, Bride, and Church.

When we mistake the promises of earthly conquest, wealth, and glory, which belong to Israel during the millennial age, and go about trying to help governments and reform societies, the Church misses its foremost calling. Again, this can be seen in the numerous false religions, false doctrines, and national actions of the world today. As with Jew and Gentile so it is with Caesar and God; we render the things which belong to each, God first and then Caesar.

During the fullness of the Gentiles our duty has been to teach, preach, report, and testify to the saving grace through Jesus Christ, yea the finished works of Christ. We are to testify one soul at a time or many. When the fullness of the Gentiles is completed the Church will be caught away, for the Body will be complete.

There is much confusion on this subject among the saints, and there should not be. Two events are in question: His coming for His saints and His coming with His saints. Let us consider the two. All of us should be able to understand that to come with someone, we first must be with that someone. If we are to return with Him, then we must be with Him. We are repeatedly told by the Lord Jesus Christ and the apostle Paul that we are not appointed unto wrath. This should not be hard for us to see. Is there proof of the rapture in the Bible?

The pre-flood prophet Enoch "walked with God and was not for God took him" (Genesis 5:21-24). Enoch was taken off the earth before the tribulation of his time. We should be able to see and at the very least consider the flood a form of tribulation.

In 2 Kings 2:11 we are told of the great prophet Elijah who, when walking with his student, was transported to heaven, "and Elijah went up by a whirlwind into heaven." No deposit no return if you will.

These are called a catching away, or being caught up, which would be a rapture event. It is all the same. As a result of these two historic events we can clearly understand that it has been done and therefore could easily be repeated. Many scriptures report the saints returning with Christ such as:

Zechariah 14:5, Colossians 3:4, Jude 14, 1 Thessalonians 3:13 and 4:14. This is a revelation or an unveiling event not to be confused or combined with the rapture.

The rapture and the revelation do not happen together and are not the same thing. The apostle Paul states many times that something is coming, a secret event. In 1 Corinthians 15:51-58 Paul explains that some will still be living and will be changed. We will not all sleep, but we will be caught up to be with the Lord. In John 11:26 the Lord Himself tells us the same.

The Law

Let us start with what the law is not. It is not the Ten Commandments! It is the "perfect law of God" (Psalm 19:7, Acts 22:3). This perfect law which was given to the nation of Israel contains not only the Ten Commandments but also 613 other laws and ordinances pertaining to spiritual, civic, and general welfare. It also contains regular observance of feast days, holidays unto the Lord if you will, all of them typing, shadowing, and pointing to the actual event: that which was to come.

Now that we know what it is not, we can know what it is. It is perfect! Just as the Lord Jesus Christ is perfect (we can research the major parts of the law in the books of Exodus and Leviticus). A major part of the law is "days to the Lord" if you will, such as the Sabbath (Exodus 20:8) and specific feast days. One such day is the Day of Atonement. The Day of Atonement (Yom Kippur) takes place ten days after the Feast of Trumpets in the New Year (Rosh Hashanah). In biblical times, this was when the high priest entered into the Holy of Holies and offered a blood sacrifice for the sins of the people.

God either accepted the sin offering or the priest died. They would then take a goat and release him into the wilderness as a symbolic gesture of removing the sin. This "scapegoat" was never to return, and thus the sins of the people would be removed from them. This atonement would cover the sins of the people for one year. We can clearly see, with some study, that no one could keep the law, for if one could there would have been no need for this Day of Atonement. We know from Solomon that "he who keepeth the law is a wise son" (Proverbs 28:7) so we must ask, who in the world is the wise son?

We know that the law is a schoolmaster. We then must ask the question: to teach what? We know from Paul that the law "works wrath" (Romans 4:15). We have a problem here; the law is perfect, but is a schoolmaster that works wrath! It also appears that no flesh can please God, "for all flesh is as grass"—it dies (Isaiah 40:6). And Paul tells us "that all have sinned and come short of the glory of God" (Romans 3:23).

"Wherefore the law was our schoolmaster to bring us unto Christ, that we might be justified by faith" (Galatians 3:24).

"Because the law worketh wrath: for where no law is, there is no transgression" (Romans 4:15).

We must understand that the law is perfect and only perfection can please God, for God is perfect. Now if God is perfect in all His ways and the living Word says He is, then He can only accept perfection. It is at this point that the believer must begin to see: that if by the law, then it must be all the law, and perfectly kept. Our Kinsman (Jesus) hath kept the law, all of it, and by faith so have we. By believing God we are counted as righteous. We are not capable of keeping the law in the natural. I beg to say we don't even know the law. Therefore how could we keep it?

The Lord Jesus Christ gives us a perfect picture of this in His conversation with some of the Jewish temple leaders.

We see clearly what He said in our own lives: if you thought it, you have done it. There is no other way to interpret what is said here by the Word (Matthew 5:22-28).

There are many "I say unto you" scriptures in the Gospels. Let the Holy Ghost convict you, for we see that to think it is to have done it. The Gospels are directed to the Jews and the nation of Israel and therefore must be rightly divided. This certainly does not limit the lessons and knowledge from them as spoken by the Son of God, Jesus Christ. All Scripture is for reproof, knowledge, and witness, and all Scripture is profitable. However, not all Scripture is to the Church nor concerns the Church. What is written and spoken to the Church does not apply to the nation of Israel or the Jew.

Grace

Here we will start with what grace is: unmerited favor, unearned favor if you will. Grace is a gift from our heavenly Father, and a free gift at that. One could call it divine mercy.

We see when God said, "I will be gracious unto whom I will be gracious and show mercy unto whom I will show mercy" (Exodus 33:19). He does not require a priest, preacher, teacher, TV evangelist, or imam to do it for Him. He seems perfectly suited for the job.

We find two such famous examples in Genesis. "But Noah found grace in the eyes of the Lord" (Genesis 6:8). And "[Abraham] believed in the Lord and He counted it to him for righteousness" (Genesis 15:6).

This is interesting, "for God is no respecter of persons" (1 Peter 1:17). Now Abraham was given righteousness as a free gift for believing God. By the way there is no record in the living Word or in history that after this gift Abraham was sinless. However there is a record that God kept His word. Therefore why would we be treated any different? Of course you do have to believe God and put your trust in Jesus Christ.

"It is better to trust in the Lord than to put confidence in man" (Psalm 118:8).

"It is better to put confidence in God than confidence in princes" (Psalm 118:9).

So we see that we should put our trust in the Father because of the Son, and thus our confidence is in God and not in any man, woman, denomination, or government. Rather it is in the finished works of Jesus Christ. Therefore in that fact our grace is good hope. We see this when Paul tells us the following:

"Now our Lord Jesus Christ Himself and God, even our Father, hath loved us and hath given us everlasting consolation and good hope through grace" (2 Thessalonians 2:16).

He consoles us with everlasting consolation which is His grace; He loves us, holds us, and provides for us all by His grace. This same grace is what will allow us to be called out before that great and terrible day of His wrath. Paul wants us to understand that the grace of God is also a throne, where we are welcome. "Let us therefore come boldly to the throne of grace, that we may obtain mercy, and find grace to help in time of need". (Hebrews 4: 16)

We are given the gift of God; the power unto salvation is a free gift. But if you do not accept the gift, as with any…you don't have it. You must receive the gift and take ownership of the gift to have the gift.

Faith

Let us start by asking what is faith? "Now faith is the substance of things hoped for, the evidence of things unseen" (Hebrews 11:1).

From this: all faith can show forth in the glory and honor that God, through the Author and Finisher, Jesus Christ, gives it. For faith is the power that we all are required to possess in order to please God.

"For without faith it is impossible to please God" (Hebrews 11:6).

God rewards our faith. In fact it seems by the Word He would prefer we put our trust in Him on a higher priority list than obedience to Him. Faith is not a New Testament concept, for true belief requires faith; it is the evidence of things unseen, "and the just shall live by faith" (Habakkuk 2:4). If faith is unseen then it is not of the flesh, yet without it we cannot please God! Therefore what is it that our faith is in? Shall it be performance, or the works of our hands? No. Our faith is in the finished works of the Kinsman, Jesus Christ.

In the Gospel of Luke we are presented with a true case of saving faith, the woman whose love for the Lord is seen in her cleaning His feet with her tears and drying them with her hair. She will not cease in kissing His feet; she has even anointed His feet with oil. Jesus turns to Simon and explains, "You have failed to do these things unto me." The Lord says her sins are many but they are forgiven, and that people who are forgiven little love little. He tells her "your faith has saved thee" (Luke 7:36-50). We clearly see that there have been no ifs, ands, or buts added to the salvation of this woman, but rather it was her faith that saved her.

There have always been questions about how to purify the heart, for the Word says God looks upon the heart. How then do we have a pure heart? We have a pure heart by faith (Acts 15:8-9). These scriptures tell us that God does look on the heart and that faith is the purifying agent used. The book of Acts tells us to "testify to the repentance of God through faith in our Lord Jesus Christ" (Acts 20:21). This is the purpose of the Church. Paul goes further when he explains:

"For if they which are of the law be heirs, faith is made void, and the promise made of none effect" (Romans 4:14).

Let us understand what is being said here. Let's step back to Romans 3:28: "therefore we conclude that a man is justified by faith without the deeds of the law." There can be no misunderstanding with what we have just read and what the living Word has spoken. If it is also by the law, then faith does not mean anything. It seems that the real problem with most believers is that we simply don't hear the truth as often as we should. More and more churches seem to spend time talking about sin rather than salvation, and more time is spent on "getting your best life now" when in fact we are joint-heirs with Christ. What good does it do to gain the whole world and miss gaining Christ and all of His creation?

Many more are moving to entertainment rather than substance. And still others teach that you must run back at every sin, and some that you must live without sin. This is the lie of the adversary, run back; you can lose it. Keep falling short and getting saved again and again until you just give up. This teaching would make Him untruthful, a liar. Yet His name is Faithful and True! We should have joy for the Word says we are more than conquerors in Christ Jesus. Paul also addressed this issue, for if we are saved by faith, then where does faith come from?

"So then faith cometh by hearing and hearing by the word of God" (Romans 10:17).

It goes without saying that sin is not to be taken lightly. For it is a curse upon mankind and must be understood: for without faith in Jesus Christ, sin separates us from God. Faith is the action of faithing it is knowing that we know that He died for us! In the letter to the Ephesians Paul gets even more to the point:

"For by grace are ye saved through faith; and that not of yourselves: it is the gift of God" (Ephesians 2:8).

We are told to draw near, get up close and personal. Take a good look at this; it is very important to us as believers. Paul wants us to look close and not miss this.

"Let us draw near with a true heart in full assurance of faith, having our hearts sprinkled from an evil conscience, and our bodies washed with pure water" (Hebrews 10:22).

"Looking unto Jesus, the author and finisher of our faith; who for the joy that was set before Him endured the cross, despising the shame, and is set down at the right hand of the Throne of God" (Hebrews 12:2).

Here we find that we are not even the authors of our own faith, but that the Kinsman-Redeemer, Jesus Christ, is both Author and Finisher of our faith. Which means He completed our faith and sits at the right hand of the Father. We can therefore conclude that by assurance in our faith we have a true heart. Paul tells us we are the joy of Jesus Christ: our Chief Cornerstone be praised! In the powerful little letter of Jude we find that our faith is holy—not our flesh, not our natural man, but our faith is most holy.

"But ye beloved, building up yourselves on your most holy faith, praying in the Holy Ghost" (Jude 20).

Faith is what God wants from us; it is how He rewards us, keeps us, and defends us. It is why we are given grace, because we believe God. And when we pray we trust the Holy Ghost for He knows what our needs and concerns are. We are built up by faith; we are not built up by our flesh or our own righteousness, but by the power of God.

Sin

Here we will look at what sin is and why. Sin is an offense in the sight of God. We then must ask ourselves what is an offense? When we are dealing with perfection (and God Almighty is perfect), we must then find the second meaning of sin. This is answered for us by the apostle Paul when he explains it is simply to miss the mark. If we combine the two we get a clear picture of the biblical defining action of sin: to miss the mark is therefore an offense in the sight of God.

This makes dealing with the sin issue very interesting. We will hear and see all kinds of condemnation out of many pulpits today professing Jesus as Lord but quite frankly denying the power of God. There are no degrees of sin and in many cases what one man feels is sin another does not. But God is the judge of all mankind, of male and female; He is the judge of all and as David explains also the judge of the issues from death, and the Word declares "therefore there is now no condemnation in Christ Jesus." If this be true are we not already in Christ by faith?

For if missing the mark is the offense then who but Christ in the flesh has hit the mark? The natural man cannot understand the ways of God. For who is His counsel? Sin is grievous to God: "and the Lord said, because the cry of

Sodom and Gomorrah is great, and because their sin is very grievous" (Genesis 18:20).

We see David requesting that his sin be cleansed so he might be washed of his iniquity. It clearly appears he is not capable of cleansing himself but rather asks to be made clean, and admits his sin and declares "it is ever before me" (Psalm 51:2-3).

The Lord speaks to Isaiah and says, "Come now and let us reason together, saith the Lord. Though your sins be as scarlet, they shall be white as snow; though they be red as crimson, they shall be as wool" (Isaiah 1:18).

In this contest the object is simple; we get one shot at the mark. The bow is the law, the arrow is our performance, and we get one shot. If we miss we fail. We must either hit the perfect bulls-eye or fail. We must perform like Robin Hood; the Lord hath placed His arrow and we must split it! We can miss by an inch or a mile, but remember what the Word has said: all have missed the mark. The Lord tells us of the woman whose sins were many and she loved much. When the Lord spoke to Paul in Acts 26 He said:

"Delivering them from the people, and from the gentiles unto whom now I send you. To open their eyes and turn them from darkness to light, and from the power of Satan unto God, that they may receive forgiveness of sins, and inheritance among them that are sanctified by faith that is in me" (Acts 26:17-18).

Let us draw near to what the living Word has said. Paul had been wasting the Church, killing, imprisoning, and oppressing the movement. The Lord strikes him blind and reveals the mystery of the Church to him. He clearly states to Paul, "When you are finished at Jerusalem you will go to the Gentiles and tell them they are forgiven and sanctified." Was it for their spotless performance? No, it would be by their faith in Him! This calling of Paul would also fulfill the prophet Isaiah as Paul would bring the Gentiles to salvation through the brightness of the risen Lord.

"And the Gentiles shall come to thy light, and kings to the brightness of thy rising" (Isaiah 60:3).

Herein are contained the basics of his job, his ministry, and his message. This in brief is the gospel of Paul. The forgiveness of sin is a free gift of God, which is provided through the finished works of our Lord Jesus Christ. Showing His victory by the preaching of His perfect life, by His blood upon the cross, and by His resurrection, and this gift is provided to all who believe. Going to the Jew first and then to the Gentile. Therefore we are one Body, one Church, and one Bride. According to the Scriptures and by the finished works of Christ, by faith, we are victorious.

To those who would profess that we misunderstand Paul's teaching we have only to look at the truth in the living Word as spoken by John the Baptist and God the Father concerning His Son, Jesus Christ.

"Behold the lamb of God which taketh away the sin of the world" (John 1:29).

"This is my Beloved Son in whom I am well pleased" (Matthew 3:17).

It simply does not say "try" to take away, He "might" take away, or even that He is "going to" take it away. It says *taketh away*; it is already taken away from all mankind but accounted to the saved by faith. In other words, when we are born again we move from a liability to an asset. We are marked "paid in full" on the ledger. The book is opened and we are checked off the list. We have in fact arrived and been accounted for. We worship a great and glorious God who sees things that be not as though they were.

To assume that the oneness doctrine, espoused by many Word-Faith teachers, holds any merit at all is broken down here by the Father Himself. He declares their relationship clearly: He is the Father and Jesus Christ is His Son. They are completely separate, one a Father and one a Son. However they have the power to be one and the same: God in Christ and Christ in God does not alter the rules by which the finished works must be performed.

As our last word here on sin, we should never pass judgment; do not say who is in heaven or who is in hell. We have all missed the mark so why argue over who is the closest? It doesn't matter. To miss is to fail. The truth is that it is hard to know someone else's heart, especially when you might not agree with their teaching. I am saved in my heart through my faith in His finished works alone. There are many who may not agree with me on salvation by faith and faith alone. Let us continue with what the Word says.

"He that is without sin cast the first stone" (John 8:7).

Almost all believers know the story of the woman caught in adultery. However it is interesting that they did not bring the man or the peeping toms with them when they delivered her. They only brought the woman to be judged; the others were let go. I have often wondered if they stopped it or watched until the two finished. But the real lesson here is this: there was one there without sin, the Kinsman-Redeemer, Jesus Christ, and He did not throw a stone.

Salvation

The most misunderstood subject in the living Word of God is the question of salvation. What do we do to find it and how do we obtain it? By what process are we to be saved, how do we stay saved, and finally can we become unsaved?

Much of the confusion is caused by men and their efforts to hold dominion over the sheep while holding themselves up. Many of them are guilty of attempting to remove the spec from our eye while having a beam in their own. Most of us have heard sermons that tell us liars go to hell, or deadbeat dads go to hell, and having a beer or smoking will certainly deliver us to doom. This teaching soon begins to sound like everything we do will send us to hell. It is odd that almost every one of these self-proclaimed prophets forgets the sins of sloth, overeating, self-indulgence, self-importance, and self-righteousness.

Some of these preachers and Internet scholars who regularly deliver such false teachings do not seem to notice their own sins. For the Word says all have sinned and missed the mark. They grow older and die just like we do; are we not clearly told that the payment for sin is death? We are told by the Word of God, "who can be against us, it is God who justifies" (Romans 8:31). We should agree that the Almighty can do it in any manner He wishes, and on any terms He chooses.

When we trust in the finished works of Jesus Christ and the Word He gave to us, we know that our sins are as far from us as the east is from the west. Why didn't He say north to south? For if you go north you will soon go south, but going east you can never go west. So as with the scapegoat our sin is never to return against us; we are free from the bondage of our sin. When we study the Scriptures, rightly divided and following the code, it seems to always declare us free from the bondage of sin. However we are not free from sin.

Some teaching goes even deeper in misunderstanding. Many of these teachers believe that the Jew can obtain salvation by keeping the law of the Torah; this is in direct dispute with the Lord Jesus Christ Himself. The Lord spoke to us on this, saying "no man comes unto the Father but by me." Therefore we should see no reason to take the word of self-appointed judges of men, but rather place our faith and trust in the Word of God, which is Jesus Christ.

So while it seems some do not consider themselves as sinners, we should in fact know we are all guilty of missing the mark. We should all have joy and peace for the living Word proclaims "that forever O Lord thy word is settled in heaven."

What does it mean this salvation? It means deliverance from destruction, so when salvation is discussed it is really deliverance from destruction. That alone kind of blows the theory of no pre-tribulation rapture, doesn't it?

Salvation is spoken of on almost every page of the living Word, David sings songs to God on the subject, and Paul preaches the greatest messages in history on the topic of salvation. That is the ultimate prize! God provides for us in the book of Job a valuable lesson when we hear of Job's faith. Despite his plight he confesses one of the greatest statements of faith we will ever hear.

"Though He slay me yet shall I trust Him: but I will maintain my own ways before Him. He also shall be my salvation; for an hypocrite shall not come before Him" (Job 13:15-16).

Job is no hypocrite; he knows in whom his salvation stands and proclaims "even if He kills me I will trust Him." This statement speaks of faith but also of our Lord. For our Lord Jesus Christ was the Lamb slain. He trusted in His Father who was His salvation, and was raised. Christ is the only person ever to live who was not a hypocrite; He kept all the law, a perfect Kinsman. David makes sure to explain who salvation belongs to when he sings,

"Salvation belongeth unto the Lord; thy blessing is upon thy people. Selah." (Psalm 3:8).

Who does salvation belong to? Not us, not our church, not our pastor, not our priest, not a saint or a mother, and certainly not some imam. It belongs to God, and He can do with it as He pleases. Now David not only knows to whom salvation belongs, but why it belongs to Him.

"He that is our God He is the God of salvation: and unto God the Lord belong the issues from death" (Psalm 68:20).

Salvation belongs to Him because He is the God of salvation. In fact He is the God of salvation and the issues from death. David goes on to explain salvation in the same manner that we learn from Paul, also of Peter, John, and the Lord Jesus Christ Himself. David sings,

"I will take the cup of salvation, and call upon the name of the Lord" (Psalm 116:13).

We hear that David is receiving his salvation by taking it; by calling upon the Lord he has taken hold of the gift. In the book of Jonah we see that the living Word of God is disclosing again whence salvation comes and from whom it flows, when Jonah says:

"I will sacrifice unto thee with the voice of thanksgiving; I will pay that that I have vowed. Salvation is of the Lord" (Jonah 2:9).

In Zechariah we read a very powerful scripture, powerful for it proclaims so much in such a small statement.

"Rejoice greatly, O daughter of Zion; shout O daughter of Jerusalem; behold, thy king cometh unto thee; He is just, and having salvation; lowly and riding upon an ass, and upon a colt a foal of an ass" (Zechariah 9:9).

Here we see not only who is to bring salvation to His people but also the manner with which He brings it, while a king, and as a lowly servant although one who is just. We also see the scripture fulfilled on Palm Sunday as the Lord entered into the city not just on an ass, but the colt of an ass, bringing salvation.

As with anything anyone brings to a party or any event, if we are bringing something we are in possession of that which we bring. When we arrive we don't charge for it; it is made available to all. Within this scripture is a powerful understanding: He is lowly as a servant. If we have employees or servants and they perform work for us, and this work is complete, did they not complete the work in our name? Is God not capable of the same? While we may at sometimes wonder who will see this salvation, we'll let the Word tell us. At some point somehow:

"And all flesh will see the salvation of God" (Luke 3:6).

While on this earth and in this life we will never completely understand how God does things, but if He says it we can be assured it has been done.

Salvation belongs to God, He has given it to the Son and through the Son and only through the Son is it given unto mankind. This is clearly proclaimed by Peter when he preached,

"Neither is there salvation in any other: for there is none other name under heaven given among men, whereby we must be saved" (Acts 4:12).

This is very clear; we are not saved by Mohammed, Buddha, the pope, Mother Mary, Allah, or anyone other than the Son of God, the Kinsman-Redeemer, Jesus Christ. Yet men and women are granted the freedom by God to choose how, who, and what they will believe, for even no belief is the belief of nothing. We continue to see and hear from the Word of God that certain facts have been spoken to us concerning His Son, Jesus Christ, that in that day no man shall have an alibi.

As one born out of due time, a man named Saul is called. On the road he is blinded, given a new name and a vision as no one else. No other had ever been given the mystery of the Church. His name is changed to Paul, a Roman name, and he is sent right back to the very people he had been destroying and on to the Gentiles to introduce the secrets and mysteries of God. The gospel will now and forever include both Jews and Gentiles into one Body, one Bride, and one Church. In the letter to the Romans Paul gives us the foundation rock of his gospel.

"For I am not ashamed of the gospel of Christ: for it is the power of God unto salvation to everyone that believeth, to the Jew first, and also to the Greek. For therein is the righteousness of God revealed from faith to faith: as it is written, the just shall live by faith" (Romans 1:16-17).

Paul explains that he is not ashamed of the gospel. Why? It is a gospel that gives no credit or glory whatsoever to mankind; it is therefore the gospel that gives all glory and power to Jesus Christ and His finished works: the cross, the shedding of blood, the Kinsman-Redeemer, and the God of salvation. He presents His perfect life, His perfect sacrifice, His resurrection, and His future return.

Are we then to put our faith in the finished works of Christ plus nothing to provide our salvation? For therein is the power of God, given to those who accept and believe this gospel and accept Jesus Christ as their personal Savior. The natural man to this day, by and large, rejects this truth. He always wants to add to it. Nothing of man can be added to His perfect work.

"God hath not appointed us to wrath, but to obtain salvation by our Lord Jesus Christ" (1 Thessalonians 5:9).

Once again it blows the theory of no pre-tribulation rapture. We are not appointed to wrath, but rather to salvation. What is the great tribulation? It is the wrath of God. Are we to obtain salvation or deliverance from destruction by our goodness or works? No! Rather as a gift of God on behalf of the Lord Jesus Christ.

We often wonder how everyone is reached with this gospel. We have clearly seen in the Old Testament the Church was a mystery. Therefore we must trust God as to how grace has been provided in the past. We need to trust the Word. As Paul tells us,

"For the grace of God that bringeth salvation hath appeared to all men" (Titus 2:11).

We now know that somehow, some way, it hath appeared to all men. The bigger question is who or what is the grace of God? The Lord Jesus Christ is the grace of God. We see that we are protected, even from ourselves, by the grace of God through faith in Jesus Christ, always holding to His finished works.

"Who are kept by the power of God through faith unto salvation ready to be revealed in the last time" (1 Peter 1:5).

Many people claim that our salvation can be lost, that it can be taken from us, and that our name can be blotted out of the Lamb's book of life. However Revelation 3: 5 is very clear, if we have overcome our names are secure by the finished works of Jesus Christ. Could they simply be limiting the power and the truth of Almighty God? Are those who would teach such doctrine both denying and limiting the power of the finished works of the Lamb of God? It clearly says "who are kept by the power of God through faith." We must therefore conclude and understand that salvation is in His power.

Atonement

The biblical definition for atonement is ransom through reconciliation. We see through the living Word that in fact this fits the Old Testament in regards to the Day of Atonement. Looking back to the Old Testament we see the example or shadow of what was to come.

"Also on the tenth day of the seventh month there shall be a day of atonement: it shall be a holy convocation unto you; and you shall afflict your souls, and offer an offering by fire unto the Lord" (Leviticus 23:27).

This was a sin offering and therefore the affliction of their soul; it was made as a covering for the people's sins of the prior year. God will add to this day later in the book of Leviticus: tenth day, seventh month (10+7=17, 1+7=8). We now understand the report; each year was a new beginning.

"Then shalt thy cause the trumpet to sound on the tenth day of the seventh month, in the Day of Atonement shall ye make the trumpet sound throughout all the land" (Leviticus 25:9).

As we know, if we read and study, the purpose of the trumpet was to sound throughout the land that all should hear. Much the same as when the Church shall hear the trump of God on the day of the rapture. Paul tells us in Romans both the event that was foreshadowed in the Old Testament and who has become our atonement when he states,

"And not only so we rejoice in God through our Lord Jesus Christ by whom we have now received the atonement" (Romans 5:11).

It is no longer a Day of Atonement, but rather through the finished works of Christ it has become *the* atonement. We receive it when we believe in the finished works of our Redeemer, Jesus Christ, always remembering in our hearts that God sees those things which be not as though they were. We are seen as complete in Jesus Christ.

Redemption

The living Word of God explains the meaning of redemption as the ransom for someone or something held in bondage. In other words a price is paid and a ransom given to get back something or someone that has been taken and placed in bondage. There was a bond placed on humanity, and a payment was required to retire the bond. The entire human race had been placed under the bondage of sin as the result of the fall of Adam.

It might be safe to assume that no one would pay a ransom for their property or children and then only redeem some of the property or only a few of the children. If we were to pay a price to redeem our property or our family we would redeem *all*, be it property or family. Then we would expect to take possession of all that the ransom paid for, leaving nothing behind. The Lord spoke through David concerning the amount and quantity of His mercy and redemption. While this is a promise to Israel it carries with it certain facts that relate to the Church.

"Let Israel hope in the Lord: for with the Lord there is mercy, and with Him plenteous redemption" (Psalm 130:7).

We see that there is mercy and plenty of redemption; neither seems to be in short supply. Both in Matthew 24 and Luke 21 the Lord Jesus Christ is explaining the signs of His coming to the nation of Israel, His revelation, and His descent to the Mount of Olives. We will use the scripture from the book of Luke.

"And then shall they see the Son of Man coming in a cloud with power and glory. And when these things begin to come to pass, then look up, and lift up your heads for your redemption draweth nigh" (Luke 21:27-28).

According to many teachers this is when the rapture of the Church takes place, which would end the tribulation; not so. The rapture is a secret event and a mystery that takes place at the beginning of the "week" not the end. This is a public event and in fact all will see. Therefore it cannot be the rapture; it is His return to save Israel, His second coming. The important thing as always is that He is the one bringing redemption. The difference here is this time the remnant of Israel will not reject their king. He will come in great power and glory and the entire world will see Him as the King of Kings and Lord of Lords.

The apostle Paul once again is where we find the truth regarding the redemption of the Church, and where we find we are already justified, and freely, when he says,

"Being justified freely by His grace through the redemption that is in Christ Jesus" (Romans 3:24).

We need to remember this. It is something we should draw nigh to. There are fourteen words in this scripture, fourteen! This is what Paul tells us in fourteen words: we are justified, we obtain it freely, it is the grace of God, and that redemption has been given to us and brought to us by Jesus Christ, because redemption is in Him. It is not waiting on anything; the Father has already placed it in Him (1+4=5).

"There is one body, and one spirit, even as ye are called in one hope of our calling. We have one Lord, one faith, one baptism, one God and Father of all, who is above all, through all, and in you all But unto every one of us is given grace according to the measure of the gift of Christ" (Eph. 4:4-7).

There is one body—the Bride and the Church; one Bridegroom—the Lord Jesus Christ; one faith—the finished works of Christ; one baptism—of the Holy Ghost; one God and heavenly Father who is above all and in all. He has given us grace according to the gift of God through Jesus Christ. We should all rejoice in the fact that it is by His measure we are given this most expensive gift. His measure is always enough for He is rich; Paul tells us why we have this gift when he proclaims,

"In whom we have redemption through His blood, the forgiveness of sins, according to the riches of His grace" (Ephesians 1:7).

His grace is rich, for we are bought not with the price of men, as in gold or silver, but rather by the royal blood of our Kinsman, Jesus Christ. He is a perfect sacrifice, thus substituting Himself as the Passover Lamb, placing His blood on the hearts of men instead of a wooden door, according to the power of the Almighty.

CHAPTER THREE

A THIRTEEN-NUMBERED CLOCK: CODE NAME FIRST AND LAST

God's Word includes history written of the past, the present, and the future. To break the code we must understand the times and seasons He is speaking of. His clock operates with thirteen locations of time not twelve. It is broken down into five ages and eight dispensations.

Before we review these thirteen positions on the clock let's understand how the clock operates. Think of the ages as hours and the dispensations as minutes, as ages will often contain several dispensations. What does it mean to be First and Last, Alpha and Omega? Let us start with explaining that God stands at all times, at the same time. He knows no time and is not bound by time. In fact we could say He is the King of Time. However the wisdom of God has given us a peak at time in His mind. What we do know is "a thousand years is as a day" to Him (2 Peter 3:8).

That means we would need to live 365,000 years to be a year old in the mind of God, so if we lived for 75 years with God we would be 27,375,000 years old. If it were 200 years with God we would be 73,000,000 years old, and for 6,000 years with God we would be 2,190,000,000 years old. Let us stop and rest on that fact. And modern scientists want us to think they understand. It has never been about the plans of mankind, the planet, or the heavens; it is about Him and His plan for the ages. For as always the earth declares His glory and the heavens His handiwork.

Let us first determine what is meant by an age. An age stands for a time between two actual changes in the physical earth. A dispensation is a probationary or moral time in world history. The living Word gives us only small amounts of information concerning the creative creation age; however we must deal with it first. It should be of note that we will see five ages and eight dispensations in the Word.

Creative Age: The Beginning

"In the beginning God created the heaven and the earth" (Genesis 1:1).

Could this be the heaven and earth before the earth is destroyed and then restored? For in the next verse we see that it was void. But you cannot void something that isn't there; you simply cannot void nothing. In the mid to late 1800s Dr. Thomas Chalmers discovered that the original Hebrew text reads "became void." Is this according to Scripture? If so we must insert something between the first and second verse. We must find the code and rightly divide the Word of truth. What information would we then have to consider, and if so what then could we have? In 2 Peter 3 we read the following:

"For this they willingly are ignorant of, that by the word of God the heavens were of old and the earth standing out of the water and in the water. Whereby the world that then was, being overflowed with water perished" (2 Peter 3:5-6).

Two things quickly: in Genesis we are told "heaven," Peter speaks of "heavens." And when the flood of Noah's time came, the earth did not perish, it was flooded. This is clearly seen by the fact that there was no need for a third creative process. Could we be looking at science and the living Word in harmony?

Could we only be seeing a limit we have placed on God? Limits of our own making? Are we failing to comprehend the unseen things of God? But if we seek, we will find for the Creator in His wisdom has given us a vision recorded in the book of Jeremiah.

Jeremiah, the great traveling prophet of God, had a vision that is recorded in Jeremiah 4:23-27. Let us read the account as spoken by the Holy Ghost through Jeremiah.

"I beheld the earth and it was without form, and void, and the heavens, and they had no light. I beheld the mountains, and, lo, they trembled, and all the hills moved lightly. I beheld, and, lo, there was no man, and all the birds of heaven were fled. I beheld, and, lo, the fruitful plain was a wilderness, and all the cities thereof were broken down at the presence of the Lord, and by His fierce anger for thus as the Lord said, the whole land shall be desolate; yet I will not make a full end" (Jeremiah 4:23-27).

Jeremiah is seeing the first earth; he is seeing it struck by a great cataclysm. The mountains are thrown down, the hills have moved, the heavens have no light. He beholds there is no man yet and tells us of cities that were broken down, that God because of His anger would make the world desolate, but not end it.

That this is not the flood of Noah is fact. For Noah did not sail in darkness, but rather for forty days and forty nights. I am sure we can agree that Noah and his family would be considered man? It is therefore clear that this is not the flood of Noah. We already know that 6,000 years to God is 2,190,000,000 years to us.

Therefore as believers we should have no problem with science taking as long as they think they need for the universe to have been created, nor the periods they require it to go through. Both on the earth and in the universe time means nothing to God. What we want is to consider the evidence presented and ask, was the earth of Adam and Eve a remodeling job, a restoration, and not the original creation event itself? We could be looking at answers to many questions if this is true. The restoration period, according to the Word, is somewhere between 5,800 and 7,000 years ago.

Now please take a minute, pray, and read Genesis 1:1. Then turn to Jeremiah 4:23-27 and go back to Genesis 1:2 and continue. Be ever mindful that in order for us to be a student approved we must be workmen rightly dividing the Word of truth.

The Antediluvian Age: Past

This is the six days of work that the living Word of God speaks of, for the Word was with God and the Word was God. It needs to be stated here that the Word of God is the Lord Jesus Christ. He is the Creator who hath created all that can be seen as well as all that cannot be seen. This age will extend from the restoration to the flood.

As we look at the Genesis account we see it is almost the reverse of the Jeremiah account, so let's draw nigh to this subject. Let the Word say what it wants to say (Genesis 1:2-31).

As we will see in the account it is a work schedule of six days. Is this six days or six thousand years? You see it doesn't make any difference, for God is not subject to time. He is Alpha and Omega, and He controls all times and seasons. His creative work is His own, and who among us can counsel Him? Here we should understand that the Word of God may be crystal clear. This most likely is a remodeling job and thus we should subscribe to six twenty-four-hour workdays.

There are interesting parts of the process to be pondered. First He creates light. This is not the sun, as it is not created until the fourth day along with the moon, but it says He made the stars also—could they have already been here? Some kind of light such as electric or nuclear was created to help restore the planet, but it was not the sun.

Then He adjusts the atmosphere and creates the firmament and again calls the firmament heaven, not heavens. Then He does something interesting; He gives a calling out to the earth: "let the earth bring forth." He is not making anything or creating anything, He is calling it forth. He is bringing something back to life by calling it forth.

Is this the first type of the future resurrection? In order for Him to call it forth it had to be there. Seeds in the earth would have survived the watery and even icy grave that the first earth was destroyed with. They would have survived to be called forth. They would have been resurrected. Again we have been given the information to prove this was not the flood of Noah, for nowhere in the account does God call forth the vegetation after the flood of Noah.

He now on the fourth day creates the sun and moon for purposes of time, seasons, days, and nights. The sun is made to rule the day and the moon the night. On the fifth day He creates the fish and the birds: He creates them after their own kind. That He did not use evolution is clear for it says "after their own kind."

On the sixth day he makes the animals of earth after their own kind. Why we even discuss evolution in this present age is a mystery to me. It is really very simple. The offspring of a jackass and a mare is a mule, and that mule is sterile. Many cross-bred bass are hybrid; they do not reproduce. In fact we see no evidence at all either in life or in the fossil records of the linking required between the two ages. However the living Word of God is clear.

He then creates man in His image; He creates male and female and in that order. The Word of God is sharper than a two-edged sword. Could we be looking at a clue? If man is to be now created in God's image, at some point in the pre-Adam earth were there men who were not created in His image? Or perhaps even men who in some limited way evolved?

He then says something that is quite easy to see, "replenish the earth." Let us ponder this, for if the earth had never been plenished we would hear "plenish the earth." But that is not what is said is it (Genesis 1:2-31).

Let's go back and look and listen. The second day, when God adjusts the atmosphere, why is it not called good? Everything else is. Could it be that once this was done Satan and his minions moved back into the earth and the surrounding heaven? For we read:

"Wherein time past ye walked according to the course of this world, according to the prince of the power of the air, the spirit that now worketh in the children of disobedience" (Ephesians 2:2).

"For we wrestle not against flesh and blood, but against principalities, against powers, against the rulers of darkness of this world, against spiritual wickedness in high places" (Ephesians 6:12).

It is clear in the record of the fall of Adam and Eve that sin was present before they were created. The inference could be that Satan and his angels were in charge of the pre-Adam earth and that the rebellion that caused Satan to be cast down from heaven brought with it destruction to the first earth. That Paul tells us "that now works" implies that at some point Satan was involved in another dispute. For the Ancient of Days, Jesus Christ, said unto them:

"I beheld Satan as lightning fall from heaven" (Luke 10:18).

In the movie trailer for *The Immortals* there is a scene that shows one of them being thrown to the earth. Could this be what the prophet saw? This event did not just happen yesterday but rather dateless years before Adam and Eve, for the serpent beguiled Eve. This tells us sin was present in the garden before Adam and Eve. The New Agers, the Dr. this and Dr. that crowd, have a serious problem here. Many of these groups will tell us there is no devil or Satan. However this is Jesus Christ speaking so we can trust what we are told. We must not park our brain with our car when entering church.

The Present Age: the Present

This period of time has been a long one for mankind. For the Lord it will extend from the flood to His second coming or revelation. For the Gentile nations it is the same, and for the Church from Pentecost to the rapture. Here we will see the start of this present age and the roots of all false religions of the earth.

"But Noah found grace in the eyes of the Lord" (Genesis 6:8).

Noah was called to build an ark. Talk about faith—it had never rained! Here it gets interesting, for Noah must trust God to perform a thing that had never happened before. So in fact Noah must put faith in the Lord to cause this new concept called rain to come to pass. The other important lesson we need to hear and see is: where was Noah's grace found? It was not found in his works, not in his life or his accomplishments, but rather in the eyes of the Lord.

"In the selfsame day entered Noah, and Shem, and Ham, and Japheth, the sons of Noah, and Noah's wife and the three wives of his sons with them into the ark" (Genesis 7:13) (1+7=8).

Let us look closely for according to addition that makes eight people. It rained for forty days, and the water covered the earth for five months. On the seventeenth day of the seventh month the ark rested (8+40+5+17+7=77. 7+7=14, 1+4=5).

It only takes about 350 years for mankind to fall back into idol worship, and Nimrod the mighty hunter bursts onto the stage of history and becomes the founder of Babylon and the first king of the earth.

"And Cush begat Nimrod: he began to be a mighty one in the earth. He was a mighty hunter before the Lord: wherefore it is said, Even as Nimrod a mighty hunter before the Lord" (Genesis 10:8-9).

The earth at this time is of one language, common to everyone. It was most likely a very difficult and extensive language, for from it came many voices. It did not take long for Nimrod to want to do as Satan, ascend to heaven and to the throne room of God. In only three-hundred-plus years man was worshiping idols and Nimrod was just like Eve, ready, willing, and able. And Nimrod wanted to be worshiped. Only the Almighty Father is worthy to be worshiped. However history shows us that the flesh of man craves this power.

It is clear that the purpose was to build a city and a tower to heaven. The Bible is very clear; while heaven could not have been reached, being governed by one man's rule and all of one accord, about anything they wanted to do could have been done. The Father, Son, and Holy Ghost go down to confuse their speech and scatter the people. Thus we have the great migration and the beginning forms of the tribes and nations of earth.

It is here that we can say: all false religions of the world owe their being to the tower of Babel. Nimrod goes on to found the city and nation of Babylon. Where it started for the first Nimrod is where it will end for the last Nimrod: Antichrist. Babylon is the place where all false religions began, and it is the place where they will all end. It is about this time that God reaches out to mankind and calls forth a people to be His covenant people, and they were to take the Word to all nations. To start this plan God calls Abraham out of Ur of the Chaldees. This is estimated to have taken place between 2100 and 2200 BC.

"And I will make of thee a great nation, and I will bless thee, and make thy name great; and thou shalt be a blessing. And I will bless them that bless thee, and curse him that curseth thee: and in thee shall all families of the earth be blessed" (Genesis 12:2-3).

The present age now has a people called Hebrews, the Jewish people, separated out and set apart from the Gentiles. From the royal line of Abraham has come almost forty-two hundred years of culture and strife, high times and low times. The Jewish people alone prove God.

Of the living Word we read today, every verse was written by Jews, inspired by the Holy Ghost. Therefore it is easy to see that all nations are able to have been blessed by the seed of Abraham. At the cross all families can be blessed through the sacrifice of Jesus Christ. This was seen by Abraham when he proclaimed "God will provide Himself, a sacrifice." At some point in the near future, upon His return, all people left will be blessed. Therefore we can conclude that while the nation of Israel has never to this point fulfilled her mission to the world, Almighty God has found great Jewish men and women who did see, just as we see: one soul at a time.

Through Isaac, Jacob, Joseph, on to Moses, Joshua, and to David and Solomon at the height of their national glory, in and out of bondage and idol worship they have remained a people. Through the rise and fall of world empires and the forming of new nations they remain. Through the rejection of the kingdom to their nation rising from the dead, God continues to use Israel for His glory and proof of His Word.

We have gone from the flood to the moon and from the wheel to the air all while this present age marches on, ever closer to the next. The entire time God is dealing with His covenant people and the Old Testament bears record to His Word, and a nation is born again to His promise.

During this present age we have seen the coming of the Son of God, Jesus Christ, and the three-and-one-half years of His ministry, death, resurrection, and ascension, and almost two thousand years of gathering out a people for His name. Not much has changed from old Nimrod through today. What we've heard all our life is true; the more things change the more they stay the same. For man has strived to build, make, and progress in his enlightenment. False worship of false gods, false worship of new gods, and some even thinking they are gods. Countless others are ever pushing God to the background, removing Him, or making Him a footnote in their teaching. As if He is going anywhere!

"For if a man think himself to be something, when he is nothing, he deceives himself" (Galatians 6:3).

But the mission of the Holy Ghost can be seen in the lives of the people who have received the truth and have put their faith and trust in the finished works of Jesus Christ. The Kinsman-Redeemer is alive today. His love is everlasting, His grace forever, and His name is Faithful and True.

This age will see the catching away of the Church, the rapture if you will. It will see the Antichrist rise to power and the formation of the old Roman Empire. It will see the false church and the time of great tribulation such as has never been from the beginning and will never be again. It will see man almost eliminated from the earth.

"For then shall be great tribulation, such as was not since the beginning of the world to this time, no, nor ever shall be" (Matthew 24:21).

This is Daniel's seventieth week, the time of Jacob's trouble. And this age will end when Jesus Christ comes to earth and saves Israel. He will restore Israel and place her at the head of the table. The Lord Jesus Christ will take His rightful place upon the throne of David.

He will lock up that old serpent Satan for one thousand years. We should understand that these things which must come have not yet come. So to those who teach that it has all been fulfilled we can by the Word dispute this. By history we know He has not yet taken the throne of David, for as we will see in the section on the covenants, it is an earthly throne and established forever.

The Ages of the Ages: Future

This is the age to come and is a dual age containing both the millennial age and the perfect age, as we will see two physical changes to the earth. One will be at the thousand-year millennial kingdom and the other will completely purify the heaven and the earth. During this dual dispensation we will also see two changes in authority and government. It is an age or time in which we are looking forward by history written in advance. It is a much more glorious earth than ever before, for Jesus will be the King of Kings and Lord of Lords, and He will remain a High Priest continually.

The Millennial Age: The Government Will Be Upon His Shoulder

"For unto us a child is born, unto us a son is given; and the government will be upon His shoulder: and His name shall be called Wonderful, Counselor, the Almighty God, the Ever Lasting Father, and the Prince of Peace. Of the increase of His government and peace there shall be no end, upon the throne of David and upon His kingdom, to order it and establish it with judgment and with justice from henceforth even forever. The zeal of the Lord of Hosts will perform this" (Isaiah 9:6-7).

As we look into the millennial kingdom let us draw nigh and look at how much is foretold in such a short space of 85 words. We cover 2,750-plus years in these two verses. We cover from the time of Isaiah through today, and in fact some time yet to come. A child was born, a son was given, and His name is called Wonderful, and by many He is considered the Prince of Peace. In point of historic fact this was all fulfilled over 2000 years ago.

Part of this prophecy is yet to be fulfilled for the government is not yet on His shoulder. He is yet to be called by all the Almighty God, the Everlasting Father. Isaiah tells us He will bring peace to the earth. We know this peace sure isn't here now. He has yet to take the throne of David, but He will. Now part of it has been done, through the birth, death, and resurrection of Jesus Christ. What must be understood is that the rest is already done, for God hath spoken it—it only awaits manifestation on earth..

When this was disclosed to the prophet Isaiah it was all history written in advance. In our timeframe it is both history completed and history written in advance, all in eighty-five words. In this age God will deal with humankind not as a whole but as nations. The Church will not be on the earth other than those who are assisting the King of Kings.

Let us now break the code of these two verses: In verse 6 we see five names used and one act He will perform. In verse 7 He presents four works He will perform and one name. Let's do the math. Five is the number of grace while one is singleness. The government will be ruled by one king and grace will have accomplished it. Four is the number for the earth, and it will be upon this earth that these acts and His government will be. And it shall be accomplished by one God, the Lord of Hosts. When these numbers are added together we arrive at 11 and 1+1=2, and two is the number of witness. He has witnessed the message within the message.

"And the Lord shall make thee the head, and not the tail; and thou shalt be above only, and thou shalt not be beneath; if thou will hearken unto the commandments of the Lord thy God, which I command thee this day, to observe and to do them" (Deuteronomy 28:13).

What are we being told? God is proclaiming that one day Israel will be above all earthly things. At this point in history this event has not yet happened. It will happen when they observe and obey His command. The whole problem with His covenant people is they have never as a nation lived up to the task, if you will. However we are clearly informed of the Almighty's intent. They will as a nation at some point see their Messiah. Why? Because God has spoken it—it is done.

As we are told in Jeremiah 31:31-37 and Hebrews 8:7-13, Israel will be under a new covenant. It will not be governed under law, nor under grace or judgment, but rather by righteousness. It will be a monarchy, with a King that will rule completely. If we read the Beatitudes we can see the basics of His government. Jesus speaking to John says,

"And He shall rule them with a rod of iron; as the vessels of a potter shall they be broken to shivers; even as I received of my Father" (Revelation 2:27).

What is the iron rod? Well let's look, what hath He received of the Father? He has received love, kindness, grace, and faith, but also power, authority, judgment, and righteousness. These are the requirements of His great Sermon on the Mount and they are met in the Ideal Man, and there is only one! This the Father hath given to the Son, and He will show Himself to mankind for one thousand years. Israel will receive their King and they shall worship their King. This will be one thousand years (one day) of peace on the earth, then Satan is loosed and once again there are people who will join him.

"And when the thousand years are expired, Satan shall be loosed out of his prison. And shall go out to deceive the nations which are in the four quarters of the earth, Gog and Magog, to gather them together to battle: the number of whom is as the sand of the sea" (Revelation 20:7-8).

John goes on to tell us Satan is destroyed; he and all who followed him are "cast into the lake of fire" (Revelation 20:10).

The Perfect Age: Eternity

That the earth is to be renovated is clear (2 Peter 3:7-13). It is to be renovated by fire. What kind of fire we are not told. But it will be a fire that purifies. It will rid heaven and earth of all poisonous snakes, plants, spirits, and pests of all kinds that had been produced by sin. It will consume the heaven and the earth and Jesus Christ will make them perfect. It is at this time that the Son presents His finished works and offers His kingdom to the Father. This is the fullness of times.

"That in the dispensation of the fulness of times he might gather together in one all things in Christ, both which are in heaven, and which are on earth; even in him" (Ephesians 1:10).

It is extremely clear that all power in heaven and earth is in the Creator Jesus Christ, and that all things will be in one, not of one, but in one. As the creative times were the beginning (Alpha), these are the ending (Omega) and it shall be a perfect kingdom. It is referred to as the eternal ages as well as the ages of ages. Marking time will cease and eternity will begin.

"That in the ages to come he might shew the exceeding riches of His grace in his kindness toward us through Christ Jesus" (Ephesians 2:7).

In the ages to come we will be shown great riches and kindness by the Father through Jesus Christ the Son. We are to be joint-heirs with Christ and yet a Bride, Body, and

Church. This is confirmed in Revelation, that eternity is come, when we hear John say that the devil, beast, and false prophet are tormented day and night forever and ever. While our concept of time will change, we know that time never ends as we are told "forever and ever."

"And the devil that deceived them was cast into the lake of fire and brimstone, where the beast and false prophet are, and shall be tormented day and night forever and ever" (Revelation 20:10).

What God the Father, Son, and Holy Ghost have planned for this age, and our role in it, we do not know. What we do know is that we are only at the beginning—eternity is very young and His love for us is eternal.

Dispensation of Innocence

As to the amount of time in this dispensation we are not told. It may not have been a lengthy time at all but it covers from the six-day restoration and creation through the fall and being cast out of the garden. Two major events take place after Adam and Eve fall. First, before they are permitted to leave the garden, the Lord God makes for them clothing.

"Unto Adam also and to his wife did the Lord God make coats of skins and clothed them" (Genesis 3:21).

This is interesting; it seems to be the first of many times God puts clothes or a covering of some kind upon mankind. It is the first time we find Him providing the proper covering in the living Word. It also sets a pattern: God is doing the work. He clothed them; they did not clothe themselves. So much for Adam being a god! As we all know if we are to get a leather coat, some animal had to die, blood was let. And God did the work. In the very next verse we read:

"And the Lord God said, behold, the man has become as one of us, to know good and evil: and now, lest he put forth his hand, and take also of the tree of life, and eat and live forever" (Genesis 3:23).

They became like God in that they knew good and evil. In no other way has man ever been, or ever will be, like God. However it is clear by the Word that they could have lived forever through the eating of the tree of life. It is He who is the Creator and Master Builder of all that can be seen or known. He is God; He is the believer's Tree of Life.

Man finds, he hunts, he gathers, he plants, and he modifies. He creates nothing, and the lie of Satan has really never changed. But the Lord God is not going to permit this flesh to live forever; it is and will always be corruptible.

The world they had known was gone; they would now work to live. They had died both in spirit and in flesh that very day. But God was already setting the type and pattern of what was to come. He performed the work to cover them before they entered the harsh world their lack of trust had caused.

There is some debate as to Eve being the first woman. Even the History Channel has put forth the idea of a woman named Lilith being created at the same time and manner as Adam, being equally created as Adam. She, through this thought, became the first advocate for women's lib. She has been celebrated with the Lilith Fair. Even women professors of Christian colleges are putting this most ridiculous notion out as if it were true. Let us unlock the mystery and see what the living Word says.

In Genesis 1 we are told He created male and female. It gives no detail but rather the order in which they were created. In chapter 2 we are given the details of how He created male and female. So we see as with any report, book, or novel it unfolds on a need-to-know basis. It is at this time mankind will be introduced to the first set of rules which are to be applied in the garden.

"And the Lord commanded the man saying, of every tree of the garden ye may freely eat. But of the tree of the knowledge of good and evil thou shall not eat of it: for in the day that thou eat of it thou shalt surely die" (Genesis 2:16-17).

That both the tree of life and the tree of good and evil were present in the garden is clear. Once again we see that sin was present, and who is the father of sin? For we see that God placed every tree in the garden before creating Adam. We know the story from here. Satan tempts Eve by misquoting the living Word and telling her:

"…ye shall not surely die. For God doth know that in the day ye eat thereof, then your eyes shall be opened, and ye shall be as gods, knowing good and evil" (Genesis 3:4-5).

It is the same lie today; nothing has changed between Satan and the natural man. But let us draw near for here is understanding. Satan lied twice; their eyes were opened to good and evil, but they were closed in their relationship to God and neither Adam nor Eve lived to be a thousand years old. A day is as a thousand years in the mind of God. So in point of fact they died that day.

We must also not miss the manner in which Satan tells them they shall be as gods. Satan is a smooth operator; he is sure not to tell them "like God" but rather as lesser gods, little gods if you will, knowing good and evil. He also says she will not surely die. Did he mean right then and there? He is sure not to mention the true Word; he leaves out "for in that day." He is smooth, he is slick, he is crafty, and he is a liar.

It is extremely important for those of us contending for the truth and those seeking the truth to be mindful of this fact. The only one who ever told man he could be a god was Satan. There is no place in the living Word of God where He or His Son, or the Holy Ghost, refers to man as a god. So when that crowd, regardless of wealth or fame, tells people they are a god, we by the Word of God can know whence the message comes.

Dispensation of Conscience

This time period extends from the casting out of the garden to the flood.

Before we start let's review the following thought. There are certain things every one of us knows about our conscience. It may produce remorse, it may produce fear, it will produce self-guilt, but it will not keep us from wrong things.

It is at this time that Adam and Eve are expected to "replenish the earth" (Genesis 1:28). No date is given for the birth of Cain, and it does not state that Abel was the second son, only that he was younger. This is not the issue God is dealing with so it doesn't matter. Cain and Abel are types or representative men if you will, Cain of the flesh and Abel of the spirit. So that we can know this is true God tells Eve:

"Unto the woman he said, I will greatly multiply thy sorrow and thy conception, in sorrow thou shalt bring forth children; and thy desire shall be to thy husband, and he shall rule over thee" (Genesis 3:16).

Eve would be putting out litters, four, five, even ten children at a time and perhaps two to three times a year.

She is told *children* and she is told "greatly multiply...thy conception."

What the living Word records is the first dispute over what sacrifice is acceptable of the Lord. Abel performs the first recorded blood sacrifice that we find, thus putting Abel in the royal line by faith. While Abel offered a blood sacrifice of faith, Cain offered the works of his hands unto the Lord. This dispute was put to the test and Abel's sacrifice was accepted while Cain's was not. So we see as far back as Cain and Able that works of the hands was unacceptable to God. *The Kinsman's Code* has started.

We are not told how much time went by before Cain's anger resulted in the first recoded murder. It ends up being a murder caused by a religious dispute, but as history bears witness it is certainly not the last.

There is not much doubt as to who was behind this killing, as Abel's faith in the blood had put him in the royal bloodline; Satan wanted to stop it. Seth, a child of promise, is born to Adam and Eve and is grafted into the royal line, much the same as the Gentile is grafted into the grace of God. Seth therefore takes the place of Abel in the royal line. Please do not confuse the royal line of grace by faith and the line of Israel. This in no wise implies that the Church has replaced Israel; at this time there is neither the Church nor the nation of Israel. However the type of faith and the pattern of acceptance for remission of sin can be traced back to this age and dispensation.

We then have three major events take place; one concerns the "sons of God" mating with the daughters of the earth. This is a strange subject and very little is disclosed about it. However it has proved to be a much debated subject. Were they really fallen angels?

We are told in 1 Peter 2:4-5, "for if God spared not the angels that sinned, but cast them down to hell, and delivered them into chains of darkness, to be reserved unto judgment." This is repeated in the letter of Jude.

"And the angels which kept not their first estate, but left their own habitation, he hath reserved in everlasting chains under darkness unto the judgment of the great day. Even as Sodom and Gomorrah, and the cities about them in like manner, giving themselves over to fornication, and going after strange flesh, are set forth for an example, suffering the vengeance of eternal fire" (Jude 6-7).

How this would be done between angels and women we do not claim to know, but it does appear to say just that. The Lord God says "of the cities in like manner"—this strongly suggests this strange flesh issue was sometime in the past. It would appear that this may have been the last straw and God then set out to judge the earth and to cause it to rain for forty days and forty nights.

In the living Word we are not told a lot about Enoch, but what we are told is that he was an important man to the Lord. He had a daily relationship with the Almighty. The Ancient of Days walked with him.

"And Enoch walked with God after he begat Methuselah three hundred years and begat sons and daughters. And all the days of Enoch were three hundred sixty and five years. And Enoch walked with God and was not for God took him" (Genesis 5:22-24).

Here we have the first recorded catching away or rapture event. The other lesson here is that Enoch is taken before a tribulation, the flood. This makes the prophet Enoch a type of the Church, saved from the tribulation of that day. Let us do the math (3+6+5=14, 1+4=5) unity of God, with man, on earth through grace. Enoch has been caught up out of the world by the grace of God. We have broken the code.

"And Enoch also the seventh from Adam prophesied of these saying, behold the Lord cometh with ten thousands of his saints" (Jude 14).

Our third event records the first spoken gift of grace being given by God to man. This shows us that grace was not a New Testament concept at all. However the manner in which grace was given in the Old Testament and the New Testament does seem to have been redirected, the shadow has become the fact. Noah looked forward, we look back — coming through faith in the finished works of Jesus Christ.

"But Noah found grace in the eyes of the Lord" (Genesis 4:8).

Let us remember once again: where was Noah's grace found? Noah's grace was found in the eyes of the Lord. We know the story, but before we close this dispensation let us remember the family of Noah. There are eight of them.

Dispensation of Human Government

This dispensation will extend from Noah, after the flood, until the great exodus of the nation of Israel from Egypt. For the Gentile nations it is still in force. Mankind will govern itself based upon how we deal with each other. As the golden rule says, do unto others as you would have done to you.

The population of the world is starting over with the eight members of Noah's family. It is during this dispensation that God will call out a covenant people and bring about the nation of Israel. Having covered the importance of Nimrod and his rebellion, Abraham and his calling in the antediluvian age, we will move deeper into the next dispensation.

Dispensation of Family

As Seth replaced Abel in the royal line and is a type of the spirit man, in this dispensation we see in the marriage of Isaac and Rebekah a type of Jesus Christ and His Bride, the Church.

In fact this is a rare event in the living Word for we have types of the Father (Abraham), the nation of Israel (Sarah), the Son Jesus Christ (Isaac), Eliezer (the Holy Ghost), and Rebekah (the Bride and Church). Remember that Sarah was barren and the Lord gave her a rebirth and she bore Isaac, a type of the rebirth of the nation of Israel.

In Genesis 24 we have the following event recorded. Abraham does not want a wife for Isaac where he dwells, so he sends his servant Eliezer back to his people to get a bride for his son. The servant finds the future bride, Rebekah. It is important to note that even though she is of Abraham's people she is not of Abraham's seed, therefore she is a Gentile.

Through Eliezer's conversation with her explaining the virtues of Isaac, she agrees to marry him, having never seen him. Eliezer places a gold earring upon her ear and two bracelets of gold weighing five ounces each upon her hands. What does this mean? The gold symbolizes the purity of the Word, and the earring upon her ear is for the hearing. The bracelets are also placed upon her. She receives the gifts; she does not have to perform any work to put them on, she has only to receive. They load the camels and off they go. As she travels to her awaiting husband, Isaac, he sees her approaching afar off and goes forth to meet her.

Let us get up close as Abraham the father sends his servant Eliezer to get a bride for his son. She accepts the witness without seeing him. When Isaac sees her approaching afar off he quickly goes forth to meet her. Have we heard of a future event like this? Yes we have. It is both a type and shadow of the Bridegroom, the Bride, and His coming in the air to meet His Bride. This types and shadows the faith of the believer, the Bride and Bridegroom, and the rapture of the Church.

We are told through this period that once again man just can't get it right. Sodom and the cities of the plain are completely destroyed. It is at this time God will start a nation and a people chosen to process the light of the world and to record and keep the oracles of God, the living Word of God.

Time after time they slip back into idol worship and false gods. Time after time God judges them. But through it all God makes His everlasting covenant with Abraham, confirms and adds to it with Isaac, and again with Jacob, whom God anoints to become Israel.

Through Genesis we see the strength of family and the disputes of family; it is like a soap opera. But through it all we see a truth hidden deep within the report. What Satan intends for evil, God intends for good. Jacob becomes Israel and a nation is born.

"And He said, thy name shall be called no more Jacob, but Israel for as a prince has thy power with God and with men and hath prevailed" (Genesis 32:28).

We see here that Jacob becomes a nation, as promised to Abraham. This is history written in advance, becoming history completed. Only the Almighty has the ability to speak history before it happens, and because He spoke it must happen.

Through a family dispute comes Joseph, the youngest but the most loved. He dreams that all the elder brothers and family will bow down to him. After revealing his dream, he finds that his elders are not happy or overjoyed with the idea. To serve the youngest, no! This is not in their plan. He is saved by Reuben from death and cast into a well, only to be found and sold into bondage in Egypt. Joseph, as later with Daniel, is given the answers to the dreams of people in high places and comes out of prison to rise to great power in the land.

He forecasts famine, he prepares for famine, and famine comes. He is correct in the meaning of the dream and rises to second in command in all of Egypt. His family comes to trade for food, and while they do not recognize him on the first visit, he knows them. Upon the second visit Joseph reveals himself to them and they recognize him. A tearful and emotional reunion takes place. They bow to him upon the second visit, as the dream promised. The family, as a type of the restored nation of Israel, bow to him as a type of Christ and he forgives them.

As stated this event types Jesus' second coming to His people in the last days. The nation of Israel did not recognize their King upon His first visit, but on His second they will. Again we see that what Satan intends for evil, God intends for good. The complete dream of Joseph took thirty-two years to come true (3+2=5), Genesis chapters 37-50. This is where the nation will be formed, during the four hundred years in Egypt; they will go into bondage and oppression under the rule of Egypt.

Dispensation of the Law

This period starts with the Passover and ends with the birth of Christ. It covers 1,491 years. God has allowed man to govern himself to this point. It is now that God, unto His people Israel, will introduce a system of government, a system for worship, a place to worship, and the assignment of priesthood.

We see the delivery of the Jews out of Egypt, as a nation by a mighty hand. God had chosen Moses, a keeper of sheep, to lead the people. The blood of a lamb shows forth as a type and shadow of the cross, the redemption and reward. Moses tells the people what the rules are to be: take a spotless lamb and kill it, place the blood on the doorposts and header, stand up, shoes on and bags packed if you will.

"For the Lord will pass through to smite the Egyptians, and when He seeth the blood upon the lintel and the two side posts, the Lord will Passover the door, and will not suffer the destroyer to come in among your houses to smite you" (Exodus 12:23).

They are all sent out of Egypt, and they all walk out free, with more wealth than was taken from them. In the book of Exodus we see the journey and the failure of the people in great detail. At Mt. Sinai Moses is given the Ten Commandments, or perfect law. Contained in the books of Exodus and Leviticus are both the social and ceremonial laws. Before leaving this dispensation let us review two important details, one concerning the law of redemption and one the event of the cross. Both will type and shadow the perfect work of the Kinsman-Redeemer: Jesus Christ.

"And if a sojourner or stranger wax rich of thee, and thy brother that dwelleh by wax poor, and sell himself unto the stranger or sojourner by thee, or to the stock of the stranger's family. After that he is sold he may be redeemed again; one of his brethren may redeem him: either his uncle or his uncle's son may redeem him or any that is nigh of kin unto him of his family may redeem him; or if he be able he may redeem himself" (Leviticus 25:47-49).

Here we have the law of the Kinsman-Redeemer and the fulfillment of the enmity between God and Satan. Adam and Eve not only sold their birthright but also the deed to the earth to Satan; God was to send His Son to buy it back. Herein are the terms: the redeemer must be a next of kin, he must be free, he must be willing to pay the price, and he must be able to pay the price. Our Kinsman-Redeemer was fulfilled in the life, death, and resurrection of Jesus Christ, the Lamb of God. He was next of kin, He was free of sin, He was able to pay the price, and He was willing to pay the price. He did this because we can't pay the price, for the price is perfection and the blood thereof.

When the nation of Israel speaks against God in Numbers 21, the Lord sends fiery serpents against the people as a judgment; many people die. Moses prays for the people and is told to put a fiery serpent on a pole, and everyone who is bitten will live if they will but look upon the brazen serpent.

"And Moses made a serpent of brass, and put it upon a pole, and it came to pass that if a serpent had bitten any man, when he beheld the serpent of brass, he lived" (Numbers 21:90).

He follows the instruction of God, makes the brazen serpent, puts it on a pole, lifts it up, and all bitten who look at it are saved. We must take careful note: there are no other requirements placed upon the people. This types and shadows the Son of Man lifted up on the cross; if we believe we are saved. For all men are bitten of sin and of the death thereof.

Dispensation of Grace by Faith

The dispensation of grace by faith extends from the cross to the crown for the Lord Jesus Christ. For the Church it is from the day of Pentecost to the catching away or rapture of the Church. This is the history of the Kinsman-Redeemer offered to all mankind, who brought the kingdom to His people, only to be rejected, and paid a price worth enough to remove every sin that will ever be committed. No refunds and no returns allowed.

As we have seen, the kingdom offered to Israel is currently on hold. He fulfills Psalm 22 as well as Isaiah 53. Jesus goes to the cross, dies, and is raised from the dead and lives so that all men may be reconciled to God; by God, through Jesus Christ. He hath reconciled Himself to man, for the power of God unto those who trust the Passover Lamb, Jesus Christ, is to be saved! This is the promised Son of David, and yet we are told to be careful here. Don't think for one minute that He will not fulfill His thoughts and purpose for the nation of Israel. Paul explains this so clearly:

"For I would not, brethren, that ye shall be ignorant of this mystery, lest ye should be wise in your own conceits; that blindness in part is happened to Israel, until the fullness of the gentiles be come in" (Romans 11:25).

We are told here that Israel has been blinded in part. It is interesting that Paul does not refer to individuals but rather to the nation. First, all the scribes of the living Word and early Church leaders were Jewish. Therefore are they the part that was not blinded? Yes. But a time is coming when He will return and the nation will see her Messiah as the conquering one they looked for the first time. Did they miss the part of the suffering Messiah? Yes, as a nation they did, so in part they have been made blind. However Paul is clear to tell us "until" which implies that at a point in time God will again address the nation of Israel.

When the Church rapture takes place at the beginning of Daniel's seventieth week, the postponement of the kingdom through Israel is halted. God will again take up dealing with the nation of Israel and the Jewish people as His covenant nation and people. We the Church, the Body and Bride of Christ, have not been dealt with under law but rather under grace. It is therefore clear by the Word that He will not forsake His people. As with Joseph, He will see them a second time and they will know Him.

"For sin shall not have dominion over you: for ye are not under the law, but under grace" (Romans 6:14).

We are never told we will not sin, for if we be honest and look upon the man or woman in the mirror, we all know don't we? But rather He tells us sin will hold no dominion over us. Why? Because the living Word explains that we are to be judged at the mercy seat, the throne of grace. When Jesus Christ sat down at the right hand of the Father, the throne went from one of justice to one of grace by faith. It is because of this grace that He will come for His Bride, just as Isaac did. It is through our faith that we will be there, just as Rebekah was. We have more proof of the rapture of the Church when we read a very seldom quoted scripture.

"I tell you that he will avenge them speedily. Nevertheless when the Son of Man cometh, shall he find faith on the earth?" (Luke 18:8).

The Church is saved by grace through faith, so faith would be on the earth, vested inside His Bride, His Body and His Church. That He would come back to earth and find no faith, well then where is faith? We are given an answer to this secret by Paul when he writes,

"For the mystery of iniquity doth already work; only he who now letteth will let, until he be taken out of the way" (2 Thessalonians 2:7).

If it is the Holy Ghost that is restraining the Antichrist then He must leave. If He must leave then the Church must leave with Him. For we were told He would live in us and would never leave us. Therefore we may conclude that if faith be gone from the earth, the Church must also depart.

It would again appear that those who teach there is no pre-tribulation rapture have a real problem. It is clear that this dispensation includes the calling out of a people for His name and the rapture of the same, but when the Church is caught out, it would seem, concerning those left behind, that this dispensation will end in apostasy, as have all the others.

We must also take heed of false doctrines that tell us God is the biggest failure in the Bible, while in fact it is clearly mankind. Both Gentile and Jew have been offered many opportunities to see the grace of God, for the earth declares His glory and the heavens His handiwork. The Almighty has never failed to show forth His glory or the truth of His creation and handiwork; in fact we are told all men have heard. So in response to such foolishness as God being a failure, the Word of God denies this. Hath He not created all? Hath He not already defeated death, hell, and the grave? Hath He not risen from the dead? He is exceedingly victorious and quite successful, not remotely a failure. On the other hand, we have all gone our own way, the way of Cain. We are the failure, not God.

Dispensation of the Judgment

This dispensation is seven years in length. It is Daniel's seventieth week. It is a time when judgment is brought to the Church, the Jew, and the Gentile. As the Church is caught out at the start of the time of Jacob's trouble, and is judged at the judgment seat of Christ, those left behind will be judged for seven years.

"For we must all appear before the judgment seat of Christ; that everyone receive the things done in his body, according to that he hath done whether it be good or bad" (2 Corinthians 5:10).

Do not be confused; the *all* are those who have been caught up at the rapture. The Lamb of God hath prevailed. He has overcome the world and those who believed and trusted in His finished works are with Him to receive the things which we have done well and bad in His Body, the Church. We are to receive reward for the handling and testimony of the Word of God. Some will have much, some little, and we may be surprised at who has the most and who the least.

If it were possible we would also be surprised at who is gone and who is left, as many will be shocked that they are still here. For the living Word tells us many will say "we did works in Your name," and He will claim He never knew them. The Word is declaring the mystery again: not by works but by faith. That we should have faith and that we should know the difference.

"Alas! For that day is great, so that none is like it: it is even the time of Jacob's trouble but he shall be saved out of it" (Jeremiah 30:7).

Here we have a simple but often missed code. Who will be saved out of it? Is it Jacob? Yes, and he is Israel. So could it read the time of Israel's trouble? Are we Israel? No we are not. And whose trouble is it? Israel's! It is so clear that He who is known as Faithful and True will return to the earth and will keep His Word; He will save Israel at His second coming: His glorious revelation. The Lord Jesus Christ will at this time judge the nations, or Gentile nations. So we see that no matter how horrible it will get there are some people left from every nation.

He will call the nations before Him and shall separate them as sheep nations and goat nations. The sheep nations are allowed into the millennial kingdom and the goat nations are destroyed. They are judged for their relationship with Israel and the Jewish people. We read the account of this in Matthew 25:31-46. The judgment of the Church will be individual while the judgment of the nations is national.

Dispensation of the Messianic King

This dispensation will extend in two parts and is also a dual age. We will see both changes in the physical earth and in the form of government. It will begin with the millennial kingdom and will move to eternity. This is both a dispensation as well as an age and was covered in the section on ages of the ages contained in the section on the millennial kingdom and the perfect age. But here we will add additional information as provided by the living Word of God. When Jesus Christ presents the Father with the kingdom at the close of the millennial dispensation we are told:

"And when all things shall be subdued unto him, then shall the Son also himself be subject unto him that put all things under him, that God may be in all" (1 Corinthians 15:28).

So we see Jesus Christ who has overcome Satan, sin, the world, restored His covenant people, purified and perfected the heaven and the earth, and completed all work. He will submit Himself again to the Father that the Father may be in all. We are spoken to by the Lord Jesus Christ as follows,

"I Jesus have sent mine angel to testify unto you these things in the Churches. I Am the Root and the Offspring of David, and the Bright and Morning Star" (Revelation 22:16).

Here we find in one verse of thirty words a period that will cover eons of time! He is the Root of David (He was before David), He is the Offspring of David (He is after David), and He is the Bright and Morning Star (His name in eternity). Let us review the math and unlock the code. Counting Jesus He uses five of His names in this statement. Therefore He has sealed it with the grace of God. Our Kinsman-Redeemer, Jesus Christ, also wants us to know He is not bound by time: He was, is, and will forever be.

CHAPTER FOUR

SCIENCE AND THE BIBLE: CODE NAME CREATOR

The Creation: The Earthly Code

While modern man has never created a thing, modern man has made more wonderful and marvelous discoveries in the past one hundred years than in the prior history of our race dating back to the flood. Our knowledge has been greatly advanced and we continue to grow in knowledge at an ever increasing and breath-taking rate.

We've come from the automobile to the airplane and on to the travel of outer space. We are most certainly going to and fro. Medicine has seen the defeat of polio, smallpox, the heart transplant, and stem cell research. The laptop computer of today has more capability than did the computer on the first moon mission; knowledge has most certainly increased. Here in this section we will take a look at the basics that all technology originated from. We will see that God has supplied the foundation and directives of all modern knowledge.

We have covered the subject related to the acts of creation in the section the creative age. What we will do here is add to that which has been disclosed.

We will take a somewhat wider view. Let us start with complete creation for the living Word gives us the following information in thirty-one words. Let's look at the math: 3+1=4. It is the earth and concerns the earth.

"The thing that hath been, it is that which shall be; and that which is done is that which shall be done: and there is no new thing under the sun" (Ecclesiastes 1:9).

Here we confirm once again that God sees those things that be not as though they already were for He declares it is done because it shall be done. What thing hath been? They are limitless, but let us look at a few examples. The earth was created perfect and shall be perfect again. The covenant with Israel hath been and will be again. The Church was in the mind of God and now is in God. This also refers to the work of Christ, for there is none other that hath been and will forever be.

There is no new thing under the sun. Think about what that really means. Nothing to God Almighty is new, not one thing. Man can find, he can discover, he can build, he can locate, he can reason, and he can modify, but everything is already here; all man does is the finding, the using, and all too often the misusing of it.

From the atom and how to split it to the electric light, the automobile, air travel, the computer age, and all the advancements in science, it has all been here forever—the oil, the gold, the silver, the sand, the sea, and the diamond. The unseen laws of gravity, energy, and mathematics have always been; they came with the creation. Within the laws of nature and of the universe, there is nothing new. This is a point we want to remember. There is nothing new in the mind of God, not in the seen or the unseen, not in His knowledge, in His creation, or in His Word.

When Moses reported the acts of restoration and re-creation he placed them in a certain mathematical order. All modern science agrees that they have been placed in proper mathematical order. Let us understand what it means when we place these eight acts in their correct order.

Moses was either an extraordinary speculator or he had "inside information." The odds are 1 in 40,320 of listing them in proper order. There are 40,320 combinations and one chance to get it right. The record of such is recorded and spoken in Genesis chapters 1 and 2 ($1 \times 2 \times 3 \times 4 \times 5 \times 6 \times 7 \times 8 = 40,320$).

That the earth in past times was dark at night is an understatement; there were no electric lights. Everywhere the heaven and stars could be seen and read. Before the flood mankind lived for hundreds of years. Thus knowledge of the heaven and of times and seasons could have been limitless. The great pyramid was built over five thousand years ago, and it is said that it could not be built today. Living for hundreds of years in good health, how much could we learn? How much would we know? So we can see that there was also vast knowledge at this time in world history. Pre-flood knowledge could have rivaled our own and in some ways surpassed it. In Genesis we are introduced to a seldom talked about man by the name of Peleg. We are told:

"And Eber lived four and thirty [4-30] years and begat Peleg" (Genesis 11:16).

We no more get introduced to Peleg than he seems to disappear. Why are we introduced to him here? It is like the Lilith question; read on, study, and rightly divide for we find him and his purpose later:

"And unto Eber were born two sons; the name of the one was Peleg; because in his day the earth was divided: and his brothers name was Joktan" (1 Chronicles 1:19).

A pretty important man, he is called the one and only if you will. And in his day the earth was divided, or measured. To divide something you must know how much you have to divide. So you use advanced mathematics and measurements. Peleg is the first man to circumvent the earth; Peleg is the one who first measured, divided, and mapped the earth. Before we proceed let's go back to the eight acts of creation. Remember the odds are 1 in 40,320: 4+0+3+2+0=9. Within this simple mathematic equation are we being told that the Creator made the earth with the fullness of blessing?

The Creation: The Heavenly Code

Let us remember and understand that we are dealing with our heaven, our universe, not the cosmos of which we have no idea how old it is or how vast space is. We currently have no understanding of the purpose or power of dark matter. We have a hard time with the understanding of black holes and their purpose. However in 1929 Edwin Hubble came to the conclusion that our universe is expanding at the speed of light. This was a major finding by science; at last they could attempt to date the earth and the universe, and for some it also provided the means to make the foolish attempt to disprove God.

While there is great skill and knowledge required in understanding the fact that our universe is expanding, simply put: you measure where a star or galaxy is today, then again at a later time, determine the distance of movement, and then calculate the speed. You then work backwards in the attempt to find the starting point. Science cannot agree on the speed required to find the exact starting date. Did it start slow and gain speed, or was it always like cats on fire? However old it is we know it is old, but not how old.

A new theory is now being put forth that at some point the universe will hit a wall and bounce back, or as a balloon just pop. We should have no doubt that these findings are heading in somewhat of the right direction. That the universe is expanding is a fact, agreed to by all. That it is to bounce back or pop is vastly limiting the power of the Creator. To date the correct age, the issue may be as simple or as complex as finding, as we have stated, the correct starting point.

But let us reason together; the planet and universe is certain to be much older than our race. How much older is the debate. The natural man found this out less than ninety years ago, discovered by Edwin Hubble in 1929. Science and the living Word must be in harmony for the living Word of God is not a dead book, it lives. It is not an outdated science book, but as with history it contains certain scientific information within itself. Let us draw near to the facts we are about to see and hear.

"Which alone spreadeth out the heavens, and treadeth upon the waves of the sea" (Job 9:8).

"Who coverest thyself with light as with a garment; who stretchest out the heavens like a curtain" (Psalm 104:2).

"It is he that sitteth upon the circle of the earth, and the inhabitants are as grasshoppers; that stretcheth out the heavens like a curtain, and spreadeth them out as a tent to dwell in" (Isaiah 40:22).

"He hath made the earth by his power, he hath established the world by his wisdom, and hath stretched out the heavens by his direction" (Jeremiah 10:12).

The living Word is powerful, logical, and revealing when it is rightly divided and fits as a perfect building, for the Carpenter is perfect. We are herein told all that we need to know; for if we read and understand, as far back as 1500

BC we were being told these facts. First: in Job we see the Creator and Son in only fourteen words (1+4=5) from the beginning unto His walking on the sea. In Jeremiah we must look deeper with our spirit and see there are twenty-five words used, 2+5=7, therefore it is perfect.

"But when they saw him walking upon the sea, they supposed it to be a spirit, and cried out. For they all saw him, and were troubled. And immediately he talked with them, and said unto them be of good cheer; it is I; be not afraid" (Mark 6:49-50).

While this is not regularly taught as prophecy we see here that He fulfills Job's statement by treading upon the sea. We are also told who spreads out the universe. He is one and the same, the Creator Jesus Christ. We are told in Psalms that His light is like a garment and He causes the universe to be like a curtain. In Isaiah more information is added. Not only does He stretch it out, and not only like a curtain, but as a tent, in fact a place for us to live. And it is very clear that the earth is round. Mohammad, over one thousand years later, thought it to be flat, like a carpet and a bed. So much for science and the Koran. Again in Jeremiah the last piece of the puzzle is placed. How He made the earth, with His power. How the world was established, by His wisdom. With what authority does the universe expand, it is expanding at His direction.

So the earth has been measured, divided, and mapped. We have properly placed the eight acts of creation. We have been told who, what, and how the universe is being managed. We clearly see here that the living Word knew that the universe is expanding, why it expands, and who expands it. While man has just now come to the knowledge of its expanding, the living Word was speaking of this and verifying it over thirty-five hundred years ago.

As we can clearly see these facts were recorded in the living Word in at least four different locations between twenty-five hundred and thirty-five hundred years before Edwin Hubble.

We see in the measuring and dividing of the earth, in the expanding universe, and the eight acts of creation that science is in harmony with the living Word of God. Therefore creation and science are in harmony and all things here were created within complete creation. We then can declare, if in harmony in the beginning then in harmony forever.

CHAPTER FIVE

THE ISRAEL AGREEMENT: CODE NAME COVENANT

We will be looking at five covenants starting after the flood with Noah and through the new covenant with the restored house of Israel. Four of these covenants deal with the Jewish people and the nation Israel. The covenant with Noah becomes a gentile covenant when the nation of Israel is formed by the call of God to Abraham. The four covenants that deal directly with Israel will all provide proof that God Almighty is not at all finished with His covenant people. Contrary to the false teaching of many; the word as we shall see is clear in relationship to this subject.

The Covenant with Noah

The covenant made with Noah is the first covenant in this present age. It contains six parts. It can be said that it is the dispensation of human government. This covenant is given in Genesis 8:29 through 9:17.

1. That God would not destroy the earth and all living things and the seasons of spring, summer, fall, and winter would continue.
2. That the offspring of Noah's family (eight) and theirs would replenish the earth.
3. That the descendants would have dominion over the earth.
4. They could now eat meat, but the blood must be drained.
5. The law of capital punishment is introduced.
6. A promise from God through Noah to never destroy the earth again by water. God gave the rainbow as an everlasting testimony to this promise.

As we understand by history, to this date the earth has not been destroyed by water and we all see rainbows quite often. It can then be assumed that to this point God has honored His Word. It is interesting that there are seven colors in the rainbow, and therefore this agreement is perfectly sealed. Most people would certainly agree we have had dominion over the earth, and the families of the earth have most surely populated the planet. This covenant does not replace the covenant with Adam but rather adds to the covenant with Adam.

The Covenant with Abraham

As we have seen the tower of Babel was a turning point in world history, from all being in one accord to the nations of the earth, seldom of one accord. The human race had again gone over to idol worship. To correct the situation God called Abraham and Abraham answered the call.

This covenant holds the basics to all others concerning the nation of Israel. These seven promises are unconditional and perfectly sealed; they cannot and will not be revoked.

They are both expanded and added to with Isaac and Jacob, son and grandson respectfully. This account can be read in Genesis chapters 13 through 35.

1. God promised Abraham that he and his offspring would be a great nation, both national and spiritual, with a land grant promised to and for the nation: Israel.
2. God promised Abraham that he and his offspring would be blessed.
3. God promised that He would make Abraham a great name.
4. God promised that Abraham would be a blessing to the world.
5. God promised Abraham (and his offspring, through Isaac) that He would bless those who bless him.
6. God promised Abraham that He would curse those who curse him.
7. God promised that through Abraham families would be blessed.

We can see that this covenant was with a new people, the Hebrew people, and not with the Gentile nations. The Gentile nations continue in the covenants with Adam and Noah. However, as we have mentioned, we see that through Abraham Christians are truly blessed.

"Even as Abraham believed God and it was counted to him for righteousness" (Galatians 3:6).

Paul explains that we are accounted to the same way, for believing the Word of God. It sometimes is so simple we just won't see it, for believing in Jesus Christ and His finished works is the righteousness of God.

"And the gentiles shall come to thy light, and kings to the brightness of thy rising" (Isaiah 60:3).

Through the line of Abraham came the nation of Israel and through Israel came the Lord Jesus Christ, and He will bless people from all nations through the brightness of His resurrection and the faith thereof. So we get a glimpse of what was to come—call it history in advance. Through the prophet Isaiah we are able to read the foretelling of an historical event and the fulfillment of the event. Today we know there are many more Gentiles in the Church than Jews. This is history written in advance and completed in our time. The dispensation of grace by faith is simply waiting until the fullness of the Gentiles be brought in and the Body of the Bride be complete.

The Covenant with Moses

This is a covenant of law and was established to be followed by adhering to the rules. This was a form of government that set both moral and civil laws in place. It also added the ceremonial law which included both the building of a tabernacle and the assignment of priesthood. It does not alter or replace the covenant with Abraham; it both extends it as an amendment and adds clarification to the purpose of the nation.

1. The moral law, the Ten Commandments (Exodus 20:1-26)
2. The civilian law (Exodus 1-24, 18)
3. The ceremonial law (Exodus 25:1-40, 38)
   (Books of Exodus and Leviticus)

Within the books of Exodus and Leviticus we have an explanation of the law; it is a revelation of the law. The living

Word explains to us the offering and the sacrifice as required for remission of sin. We are shown the Day of Atonement, the rules of the Kinsman-Redeemer, and the purposes behind both. This covenant was in force until Titus destroyed the Temple in 70 AD and is postponed at this time. In the near future these laws and feast days will be returned to Israel, and the covenant will be put back in force at the time of the seven-year peace treaty between Israel and the Antichrist.

The Covenant with David

The covenant with David was delivered in a different manner. It was delivered to David through Nathan the prophet at Jerusalem. It contains four promises. These promises are a covenant of what is to come through the offspring of David. They are history in advance and cover to date around three thousand years and counting. These four promises concern the generations that are to follow King David. The record of this covenant is contained in 2 Samuel 7:4-17.

1. God promised to establish the house of David
2. God promised to establish the throne of David
3. God promised to establish the kingdom of David
4. God promised to establish the everlasting kingdom of David

We should notice there are four promises, and four is the number of the world or earth. Therefore we see in the account that God promises David a royal house that will never be destroyed; it will never end and it is an earthly kingdom. This alone sets aside the false teaching that the Church has replaced the Jew. This is not possible for the Church is never promised an earthly kingdom.

"He shall build an house for my name, and I will establish the throne of His kingdom forever" (2 Samuel 7:13).

We know the earthly kingdom is on postponement. Since the captivity of 606 BC only one king has been crowned, and He with a crown of thorns. We see in Psalm 72:1-20 that the future kingdom will be of this world, and that the Son of David will possess a kingdom that goes from sea to sea and from the river to the ends of the earth. Therefore it cannot be Solomon's kingdom as it never extended to the ends of the earth. This kingdom is yet to come. We are told in Luke the following:

"He shall be great and be called the Son of the Highest: and the Lord God shall give unto Him the throne of His father David and He shall reign over the house of Jacob for ever: and of His kingdom there will be no end" (Luke 1:32-33).

It is explained to us so clearly that David has been promised an heir to the earthly throne of Israel. And this kingdom has been promised to have no end; it is forever. To the many who teach that God has abandoned His covenant people and that the Church has replaced Israel, I declare by the living Word that this is not possible. It simply cannot be. God will never cancel a covenant or break His Word, for His Word will never pass away. Men and women, young and old, TV preachers, popes, and ayatollahs alike will all break a deal, but not Almighty God, for as it is written: "forever O Lord thy word is settled in heaven."

The Covenant with Reborn Israel

This is a covenant that has yet to be made, but will be made with Israel when they are back in their land and have been delivered from the time of Jacob's trouble; it is therefore a millennial covenant. It will not eliminate or void the covenant with Abraham, Moses, or David but rather explain it and add to it, and of course fulfill it.

"Behold, the days come, saith the Lord, that I will make a new covenant with the house of Israel, and with the house of Judah" (Jeremiah 31:31).

At some point in the near future the Lord is going to make a new covenant with both Israel and Judah. When reading the entire context (Jeremiah 31:31-34) we understand that this is not the same as with their fathers when He brought them out of Egypt. Rather, it is a new covenant; He makes this covenant with the House of Israel or the nation restored. They will have His laws written in their hearts: they will know Him, and He will, as with Joseph, forgive His people and they will worship Him forever.

"I delight to do thy will, O my God: yea, thy law is within my heart" (Psalm 40:8).

CHAPTER SIX

THE SECRET LANGUAGE OF GOD: CODE NAME MATHEMATICS

Mathematics: The Code

The Almighty God speaks to us in many ways. The use of mathematics within Scripture as we have seen is a vital matter within His Word. Therefore we have the secrets to the understanding of His Word. The fact that they are secrets never implies that they can't be found and understood. But rather it requires work. Study to show thyself approved, rightly dividing the Word of truth.

When we study the living Word we must trust the Holy Ghost, and when we see numbers used we must look closely to find if there is a reason they are used. Certain numbers appear in Scripture more often than others, such as three, five, seven, eight, nine, and forty. They can carry both witness and insight to the text. Here we will list the most widely used numbers and their meaning and provide scriptures to support and explain each number.

1 - The primary number: deity, singleness (Exodus 4:4-6, Deuteronomy 6:4, Ephesians 4:4-6)

2 - The number of witness and testimony (Genesis 1:16, 19:1; Exodus 25:22, 31:18; Numbers 4:16; Deuteronomy 17:6; Joshua 2:1; Matthew 26:6; Luke 24:4; Acts 1:10; Hebrews 6:18; Revelation 11:3)

3 - The number of unity, accomplishment, universe: universe (space, matter, time), space (height, breadth, length), matter (energy, motion, phenomena), time (past, present, future), and of course Father, Son, and Holy Ghost (Genesis 6:10, Joshua 1:11, Judges 7:22, Ezra 10:9, Esther 4:16, Jonah 1:17, Luke 13:7, John 2:19)

4 - The number of earth such as north, south, east, and west; seasons as in winter, spring, summer, and fall. Fourfold ministry of Christ: king, servant, perfect man, and mighty God (Daniel 7:3, Matthew 13, Revelation 6)

5 - The number of grace (Leviticus 1-5, 26:8, 1 Samuel 17:40, Matthew 14:17, 25:2)

6 - The number of man (Genesis 1:31, Numbers 35:6, Joshua 6:3, 1 Samuel 17:4, Daniel 3:3, Revelation 13:18)

7 - The number of God and divine perfection: there are seven sayings on the cross, seven miracles in the Gospels, seven seals, trumpets, and bowls (Genesis 2:2, Psalm 12:6, Daniel 9:24, Matthew 18:22, Revelation 1:4, 12, 16, 5:1, 8:2)

8 - The number of new beginning (Genesis 7:13-23, 17:12; John 20:26)

9 - The number of blessing (Genesis 17:17, Romans 12, 1 Corinthians 12, Galatians 5:22-23, Ephesians 4)

10 - The number of human government and authority (Ruth 4:21, 1 Kings 11:31-35, Daniel 7:24, Revelation 17:12)

12 - The number of divine government (Genesis 49, Matthew 10, Revelation 7, 21)

30 - The number for sorrow and mourning (Numbers 20:29, Deuteronomy 34:8)

40 - The number of trial, testing, and judgment (Genesis 7:4, 7:12; Exodus 3, 24:18; Numbers 13:25, 14:33; 1 Samuel 17:16; Jonah 3:4; Matthew 4:2; Acts 1:3)

50 - The number of ceremony, celebration, and jubilee (Leviticus 15:15-16, 25:10-13; 2 Samuel 15:1; 1 Kings 1:5; Acts 1)

70 - The number of human committees and judgment (Numbers 11:16, Isaiah 23:15, Jeremiah 29:10, Daniel 9:24, Luke 10:1)

Mathematics: The Language

We have a list of the most used numbers that add to the teaching of Scripture. Today we hear a lot about the Bible code; well here is a code, a language that speaks loud and clear from the Great Mathematician Himself unto us His students. His use of numbers both enriches and adds great understanding to the living Word of God.

"Hear, O Israel: the Lord our God is one Lord" (Deuteronomy 6:4).

This is explaining that they are two but one; in the record of Paul (Ephesians 4:4-6) we have the Spirit added, and the three are one...ONE

"And He gave unto Moses, when He had made an end of communing with him upon Mt. Sinai, two tables of testimony, tables of stone, written with the finger of God" (Exodus 31:18).

That the law was brought to Israel by two, God and Moses, and written on two tablets of testimony lets us understand they are both testament and witness...TWO

"And Noah begat three sons, Shem, Ham, and Japheth" (Genesis 6:10).

Here you have three as in three sons that will go with Noah and their wives, which are three, thus family unity is preserved...THREE

"And four great beasts came up from the sea, diverse one from another" (Daniel 7: 4).

Here we see the number refer to four earthly kingdoms and establish that it is related to the earth...FOUR

"And he took his staff in his hand, and chose him five smooth stones out of the brook, and put them in a shepherd's bag which he had, even in a scrip; and his sling was in his hand: and he drew near to the Philistine" (1 Samuel 17:40).

There is so much here it is almost too much. First he has the staff; who is the staff of life? Second he picks up five smooth stones without blemish and puts them where—into the shepherd's bag. We see here that the grace of the Shepherd is what delivered the giant into the hand of David...FIVE

"Here is wisdom. Let him that hath understanding count the number of the beast: for it is the number of a man; and his number is six hundred three score and six" (Revelation 13:18).

This one is easy; he is a man and that is verified by the 666, so we have established that it is the number of man...SIX

"The words of the Lord are pure words; as silver tried in a furnace of earth, purified seven times" (Psalm 12:6).

His words are pure why? They have been tried seven times in the furnace and are pure, perfect...SEVEN

"In the self same day entered Noah, and Shem, and Ham, and Japheth, the sons of Noah, and Noah's wife, and the three wives of his sons with them, into the ark" (Genesis 7:13).

We see very clearly here that after the flood God is establishing a new beginning with eight people...EIGHT

"Then Abraham fell upon his face, and laughed, and said in his heart, shall a child be born unto him that is an hundred years old? And Sarah that is ninety years old, bear?" (Genesis 17:17).

How will the nations, the families, and Israel be blessed? Ten times nine through Abraham to Isaac, Jacob, and all nations richly...NINE

"And he took ten men of the elders of the city, and said, sit ye down here. And they sat down" (Ruth 4:2).

These chosen men were to judge Ruth in the book of Ruth...TEN

In the chapters given for the number twelve we see that we have twelve tribes, twelve apostles, and there will be twelve gates and twelve foundations in the city New Jerusalem (Genesis, the four Gospels, and Revelation)... TWELVE

"And when all the congregation saw that Aaron was dead, they mourned for Aaron for thirty days, even all the house of Israel" (Numbers 20:29).

"And the children of Israel wept for Moses in the plains of Moab thirty days: so the days of weeping and mourning for Moses were ended" (Deuteronomy 34:8).

This establishes the number thirty as related to mourning and sorrow...THIRTY

"For yet seven days and I will cause it to rain upon the earth forty days and forty nights; and every living substance that I have made will I destroy from off the face of the earth" (Genesis 7:4).

"And Moses went into the midst of the cloud and gat him up into the mount: and Moses was in the mount forty days and forty nights" (Exodus 24:18).

"And when he had fasted forty days and forty nights, he was afterward an hungered" (Matthew 4:2).

"To whom also He shewed himself alive after His passion by many infallible proofs, being seen of them forty days, and speaking of the things pertaining to the kingdom of God" (Acts 1:3).

Within these four scriptures we see the number forty used to pass judgment upon the earth. We see it used for Moses to receive the law. We see it for Jesus Christ to be tried and tempted. We see it for the risen Lord to preach the kingdom of God, to prepare His disciples for His ascension, and to prepare His disciples for the coming day of Pentecost. We see it to teach the anointing of the Holy Ghost and the starting of a people for His name, the Church...FORTY

"A jubilee shall the fiftieth year be unto you: ye shall not sow, neither reap that which groweth of itself in it, nor gather the grapes of it in thy vine undressed. For it is the jubilee holy unto you: ye shall eat the increase thereof out of the field. In the year of this jubilee ye shall return every man unto his possession" (Leviticus 25:11-13).

"Until the day that he was taken up, after that He through the Holy Ghost had given commandments unto the apostles whom He had chosen" (Acts 1:2).

We hear the nation of Israel is to have a jubilee or a celebration every fifty years and that everyone is returned to his possession. This is a shadow of what was to come, as Adam lost the possession, Christ took it back and at Pentecost provided our possession, rightness with God, to us by the power of the Holy Ghost as a result of grace by our faith...FIFTY

"And the Lord said unto Moses, Gather unto me seventy men of the elders of Israel, whom thou knowest to be the elders of the people, and officers over them; and bring them unto the tabernacle of the congregation, that they may stand there with thee" (Numbers 11:16).

"After these things the Lord appointed other seventy also, and sent them two by two before His face into every city and place, whither He would come" (Luke 10:1).

Here we see that seventy men were appointed by Moses and that this also is a shadow of that which was to come, and which did come when Jesus Christ appointed seventy also. The committee was formed...SEVENTY

Through the use of numbers God not only speaks to us but also provides witness to us. His living Word is correct, true, and alive. His use of numbers also has another important purpose: to rightly divide the Word of truth; it magnifies the report. God wants us to know certain truth. Let us draw near to the historical report of David and Goliath once again.

Goliath stood between 10 and 11 feet tall and would have tipped the scales at about 675 to 750 pounds. His coat of mail weighed 169 pounds. His staff is compared to a weaver's beam, about 18 feet tall and 6 inches in circumference; the spearhead weighed 19 pounds. In full battle attire he would have weighed between 1,100 and 1,200 pounds.

Not good odds for a teenage shepherd boy with a staff, a shepherd's bag, five smooth stones, and a sling, weighing in at about 150 pounds. If this fight were in Las Vegas the odds would be about a million to one!

The giant had taunted Israel for forty days, thus taunting, tempting, and testing God. David is told to take his staff, but he is not going to use it. He is told to get five smooth stones; not just stones, but smooth stones; not one, two, three, or four but five—he'll only use one. He is told to put them in his shepherd's bag. He is to take his sling. What now are David's assets?

He has five smooth stones (the grace of God), a staff (the Father), a shepherd's bag (the Son of God), and a sling (the Holy Ghost).

We see and hear that David was delivered by the grace of God (5), that with him were the Father, Son, and Holy Ghost (3), and that this was a new beginning for Israel (5+3=8). David, a shepherd, would rise to the office of the king and the royal line through which Jesus Christ would come would now be established.

Mathematics: The Ancient Witness

"In that day shall five cities in the land of Egypt speak the language of Canaan, and swear to the Lord of hosts; one shall be called, The city of destruction. In that day shall there be an altar to the Lord in the midst of the land of Egypt, and a pillar at the border thereof to the Lord. And it shall be for a sign and for a witness unto the Lord of hosts in the land of Egypt" (Isaiah 19:18-20a).

Let us first answer the riddle contained herein for us. How are we at the border and yet in the middle? During Egypt's history the land had been governed by a pharaoh or a pair of pharaohs. When it was divided into upper and lower Egypt it was divided at the Great Pyramid. Thus the pyramid is both on the border and in the middle. And the riddle is solved. There is no other structure on the planet that could fit this riddle.

Verse 19, when assigned the Hebrew language and converted to the numeric value, renders 5,449. The pyramid is 5,449 inches tall (5+4+4+9=22, 2+2=4) and is four-sided. It is built on solid rock and covers 13 acres (1+3=4). Its four sides are perfectly aligned to the points of the compass. It is located in the center of the earth. The pyramid was not built to be a tomb. There are no drawings or markings of any kind on the inside of the building, save a circle on the upper inside relief. It was built using the sacred Hebrew cubit, 25.025 (2+5=7, 7+7=14, and 1+4=5).

Contained in its measurement is the equation for Pi, 3.14159, approximately 5,500 years before man would find this mathematical equation. Its sides are 365.2422 cubits, equal to the days in a solar year even allowing for the leap year.

The angle of the slope is 10 to 9, or as you go up the slope 10 feet you go up 9 feet in height. If you then multiply the height by 10 to the 9th power you get 91,840,000, which in miles is the distance of earth at its closest point to the sun.

The capstone was not used by the builder; it was never installed. It is thus that the builders rejected the chief cornerstone or capstone. It was built with a covering of 144,000 perfectly matching pieces of polished limestone. It would have shone forth like a star from the rays of the sun on the flat plains of Egypt.

The Great Pyramid is said to be aligned today after almost fifty-five hundred years, closer to due north than the Paris observatory. It is the only one of the seven ancient wonders of the world still present. Let us allow some thought here for this is knowledge. At one time there were seven wonders; six are gone. Is it odd that six is the number of man and seven the number of God's perfection? Could it be saying to us that man's buildings have been thrown down while His wonder remains to be understood in that day?

In feet the pyramid is right at 455 feet tall, the approximate average height of the earth above sea level (4+5+5=14, 1+4=5). These mathematical facts represent a very small amount of information on the Great Pyramid of Giza yet we see that this structure was engineered by a divine architect and required an earthly builder with divine wisdom.

Before we take a very quick yet fascinating tour let us look at one feature of this structure. Most of us should be familiar with the number 144,000. In Revelation 7:3-8, this is the number of the sealed servants of Almighty God from the 12 tribes of Israel, and they will preach again the message of John the Baptist. They will proclaim to all the corners of the earth the kingdom of heaven is at hand and will testify to many unto salvation.

We should find it interesting that the pyramid builder covered the exterior with 144,000 precise pieces of polished limestone, the same number of precise servants as the Lord will send forth as witnesses in the last days. They will most surely offer a new beginning to those who are left behind (1+4+4+0+0+0=9).

Let us go deeper into this witness of stone. In 1839 Sir John Herschel calculated that the polished rum lines which lead to the opening lined up to the North Star, and his calculation brought him to 2170 BC as the construction date. However many believe the pyramid to be much older, as do I. I believe the builder was the prophet Enoch, and therefore the pyramid would pre-date the flood. According to certain Christian archeologists the date Herschel found was most likely the starting point for dating the prophecy contained in the structure. It is interesting that we may be looking dead-on at the actual date for the call of Abraham.

The North Star in 2170 BC would have been Alpha Draconis or star of the dragon. The North Star today is Alcyone, star of the Savior. By calculating the two you have the confirmation and therefore the starting date for the information hidden within the structure. This information is calculated as one inch per year. When using this method many students of the structure have found the correct dates of the exodus from Egypt, the birth and crucifixion of our Lord

Jesus Christ, and the ministry of Paul. The rum lines used also cross the Red Sea, the River Jordan, and the little town of Bethlehem. When we look with wisdom, this must be by design. There are many human events also located using this same method, such as World War I, the Great Depression, World War II, and many others.

Most of us are familiar with the progression of the equinox; a star that is located at a certain point today will be at this same location again in 25,827 years. When the base of the pyramid is added together we get 25,827 inches. So if you measured from one corner around the building and back to the starting point you would go 25,827 inches. There seems to be much more here than a tomb, which has never held a body. It would seem that the builder or contractor of this great wonder had inside information.

As we have seen the Almighty will use both complex and simple equations to provide proof to His report or add insight. Let us look at the code we've been given and unlock a secret or mystery. When you add 2+5+8+2+7=24 and 2+4+6, then 25+8+2+7=42 and 4=2–6 then 258+2+7=267 and 2+6+7=15 and 1+5=6 and finally 2582+7=2589 and 2+5+6+9=24 and 2+4=6, no matter how you add it up it will always end in 6. There are five ways to add this from front to back, as we have done, and we see by the grace of God the information He wants us to know.

First we are being told who built it for six is the number of man. Therefore we are also being told who did not build it. Aliens did not build it. We can dispel that thought forever. The Creator has stamped the needed information; the contractor and builder was a man. Let's go back now to the living Word of God. Let's unlock the secret and see if it was built by a contractor with the instruction and blueprint of the Ancient of Days, or if the ancient Egyptians built it.

"Jesus said unto them, did ye never read in the scriptures, the stone that the builders rejected, the same is become the head of the corner: this is the Lord's doing and is marvelous in our eyes?" (Matthew 21:42, Mark 12:10).

The first thing to notice is that a head of the corner or chief cornerstone can only exist at the top of a four-sided pyramid. Second, the builders of the pyramid did not use the capstone and thus the builders rejected it. Third, in whose eyes was He speaking? Could He be making reference to the eyes of God the Father, Son, and Holy Ghost, therefore our eyes?

"Unto you therefore which believe He is precious; but unto them which be disobedient, the stone which the builders disallowed, the same is made the head of the corner" (1 Peter 2:7).

What we are being told here for the third time is as follows: Israel has rejected her King and the one they rejected has become the head of all things, and all things are placed under Him. The chief cornerstone is always located at the top; therefore all things would be placed under it.

"And are built upon the foundation of the apostles and prophets, Jesus Christ Himself being the chief corner stone" (Ephesians 2:20).

Paul always has a way of getting right to the point. Here the living Word speaks out loud. Jesus Christ is the Chief Cornerstone, there is no debate. God disclosed unto Paul certain "things of God" that we were not allowed to know. Paul claims that it would be "unlawful" for him to speak of these things. Here we now know that the Great Pyramid is much more than the wisdom of this world can admit. It is an ancient witness to the one true God.

To take a tour of the inside and the mathematics involved would take volumes and volumes, and they are out there to be found. But for now let's cover a few highlights. First, if the Egyptians built it, why didn't they know how to get inside it? They did not know where the door was.

It wasn't until 820 AD, about thirty-five hundred years later, that the opening was found, after much searching and quite by accident. The inside tunnel descends at an angle, and at a certain point you reach an ascending passage (that was at one time blocked by a large stone). Until the large stone was removed you could not ascend up the passage to the Grand Gallery, which leads to the Queens and Kings Chamber. This could be a clue. For mankind cannot ascend to God without the weight and burdensome stone of sin being removed.

At a certain point up the ascending passage you reach the Grand Gallery. One entryway goes to the Queens Chamber, and on up the passage is the Kings Chamber, where there is an empty coffin with the stone lid removed. This would seem to point us to the tomb of Christ, which we know is also empty for the stone hath been removed. Is it speaking to us, placing the Queens Chamber as the nation of Israel, the earthly kingdom, and the Kings Chamber as the heavenly kingdom?

Going back to the descending passage and continuing down to the pit, part of the way down we find a passage bursting upward to enter the Grand Gallery. Could we be looking at Christ descending to the heart of the earth and busting forth, overcoming death, hell, and the grave?

What we have learned by the great men who have studied this marvelous wonder is: using the code of one inch per year, and following the passages, we can date the exodus from Egypt, the birth of Jesus Christ, the ministry of Jesus Christ, and the preaching of the apostle Paul. We can cross the Red Sea, the River Jordan, and journey into the birthplace of Jesus Christ, the town of Bethlehem.

As previously stated, many other events are recorded in both the living Word of God as well as the pyramid pertaining to both biblical and world history. It is truly an ancient witness made of solid rock. I have greatly simplified the information, and that's an understatement. I pray you will investigate on your own.

However we must look at these last few pieces and put them together in their place. A man named Peleg measured, divided, and mapped the earth. After the flood the building site of this great structure was located in the center of all land mass and aligned with the points of the compass upon solid rock. Therefore Peleg would have had the perfect location from which to both start and complete his work.

Almighty God would have needed a man of great knowledge, someone who the Almighty could trust and count on. The most likely contractors are: Shem, Job, or Enoch. As stated my choice is Enoch, after having studied the book of Enoch, which is quite an amazing book; for like Isaiah Enoch sees from Alpha to Omega. The prophet Enoch is quoted in the living Word on several different occasions. He lived 365 years. The only carving in the pyramid is a circle representing 365 days in a solar year, 360 days a year as the biblical year, and 360 degrees in a circle.

The last reason is "for God took him." Could he then be the one with the knowledge to contract the job? Enoch walked with God...what on earth would they have discussed? The weather? If someone had been given that much knowledge and his work was complete, it might be wise to get him out of there. Likewise when the Son of God had finished His work He also was taken up. I am certainly not alone in this opinion.

Therefore we may say: there is no other building in the world nor ever has been that answers the riddle and contains the history, science, astrology, mathematics, and prophecy built inside its measurements. It contains knowledge that would not be known for about forty-five hundred years. This is only possible by divine design, and it was built as a scale model of the earth and a witness to the living Word. Isaiah clearly states "in that day it shall be a witness unto the Lord of hosts," and it is to be understood as such.

We are now allowed to see how much depth and information God provides for us. Through the use of numbers and mathematics He has created a code that both confirms and witnesses a vast amount of knowledge contained in the Word of God and within this great structure. The vast majority of the world would like us to believe that the Great Pyramid was built by the Egyptians and that an ancient king of Egypt was the contractor. While we should have no doubt they were great builders, and history has shown us this, we can clearly see that in this case the world is wrong; for the natural man knows not the things of God.

Let us take a very brief look at the Sphinx; could it be the face of a woman and not a man? Does it not also have the body of a lion? Could it be saying Virgo the Virgin and Leo the Lion? Was our Lord not born of a virgin and is He not the Lion of the Tribe of Judah? Perhaps there is a little secret here also. Food for thought isn't it.

CHAPTER SEVEN

SECRETS OF THE FUTURE: CODE NAME TYPES AND SHADOWS

To give more understanding let us look at what types and shadows are. A type is a person: we are of similar type, or he's a lot like me, and they're almost alike. It can also be a type of a future event, of the cross, resurrection, and salvation concerning Jesus Christ, the Church, Israel, and Gentile nations. A shadow is similar but is more in line with an image of some future event; it casts a shadow of the real thing, without the substance.

A good example would be the story of the Passover in Exodus 12. Let us review the account. The Israelites are to take a spotless lamb, kill it, take blood and hyssop, and mark the head and the post of the door; they are to eat the lamb standing up and ready to go. When the angel of death comes he passes over the houses that are blood-covered. They are saved from the death of this event. As a result of this finial plague Pharaoh lets them go, richer than when they got there.

The spotless lamb is a type of Jesus Christ. The blood placed on the door is a shadow of the cross and Pharaoh is a type of Satan. Leaving Egypt richer than when they came in is a type of the rapture and a shadow of the restoration of Israel. For we certainly leave richer than when we came in, and Israel will be above all nations in the millennial kingdom.

Types and Shadows of Christ

We are going to look at a few of the types of Jesus Christ, the Savior. We must understand these are but a very few examples. It is safe to point out that every great man of faith we meet within the Word types Him in some amazing or even supernatural way.

"Yet now, if thou wilt forgive their sin—; and if not, blot me, I pray thee, out of thy book which thou hast written" (Exodus 32:32).

Here we see Moses offer himself as a sacrifice for the people's sin. He will give up his own life in exchange for the people; even after all their unbelief and all they had done, he will give himself a ransom for the people, and he does so with no exceptions and without conditions.

"Now the Lord had prepared a great fish to swallow up Jonah. And Jonah was in the belly of the fish three days and three nights" (Jonah 1:17).

"For as Jonah was three days and three nights in the whale's belly, so shall the Son of Man be three days and three nights in the heart of the earth" (Matthew 12:40).

Here we have the shadow and the image, but also the type almost side by side. First, was Jonah in the belly of a fish for three days and three nights? Darn right he was. Jesus Christ tells us he was. He is witnessing the living Word. This was not a story but an actual historic event.

The first type is Jonah and Jesus Christ; they are both in a belly if you will. They are both gone for three days and three nights. This is a shadow cast from the real events of Christ. While Jonah is a type of the resurrection we have no information ever reporting his death. However, as with Lazarus, we may consider that he may have died and then was spoken back to life. There could have been a three-room apartment for all we know. It types and shadows the real event: Christ died and three days later was resurrected.

Reading the whole story, Jonah was sent to Nineveh, a Gentile city. After the day of Pentecost where did Jesus send Paul? To the Gentiles! Look at the depth here; Jonah is also a type of Paul, a Jew sent to preach salvation to Gentiles.

"And Melchizedek king of Salem brought forth bread and wine: and he was the priest of the most high God" (Genesis 14:18).

"For this Melchizedec, king of Salem and priest of the most high God, who met Abraham returning from the slaughter of the kings and blessed him; to whom Abraham gave a tenth part of all; first being by interpretation King of righteousness, and after that also King of Salem, which is King of peace; without father, without mother, without descent, having neither beginning of days, nor end of life; but made like unto the Son of God; abideth a priest continually" (Hebrews 7:1-3).

Draw near; see what we see, and hear what we hear: Melchizedek is quite a man. Exactly who is he? Let us listen to what the living Word says. He is made like unto the Son of God, He is without father, without mother, and without descent. He has no beginning of time; He has no end of life.

He receives one-tenth; He brings both bread and wine. And He is the High Priest of the Most High God continually!

Here we have the Son of God being a type of Himself. No beginning and no end: God, first being by interpretation King of Righteousness by the Holy Ghost. He brings bread and wine, a shadow of the Last Supper. He is King of Peace and a High Priest of the Most High: He is Jesus Christ.

We can confirm this within the text. He uses five names (grace) seven times (perfection).This is not the only visit the Son of God makes to earth before His birth as a man. We see that they are a type when we understand; He has yet to have been born of a woman, as a kinsman: to age as us, eat as us, sleep like us, and do all manner of things like us. To both laugh and cry like us. He would be tried like us but not fail like us. He felt pain and heartache much more than us. For the Creator was going to die for the creature. His visits in the Old Testament are as many as His names, and He took whatever form He wanted. But He came once as the Kinsman-Redeemer to die for man!

Before closing let us look at the information concerning Lot, and also of David. Does not the Lord go to Sodom, find Lot, and take him out from Sodom before it is destroyed? On the way out they are told not to look back. But Lot's wife loved Sodom and she looks back. She is turned into a pillar of salt; her love for this world was why she disobeyed God. Now the other three came out and were saved. Not because they were perfect, but rather as a promise to Abraham. Much in the same manner as the Father has promised to give the heathen or Gentile to the Son. And they trusted God and were saved as we will be saved by the same manner, by trusting in the finished works of Jesus Christ. If that is not a type and shadow of the catching away or rapture, I don't know what is. He is marvelous in His ways.

Once again to David: was he not a keeper of the sheep, and did he not ascend to the throne? Did not the Lord Jesus

Christ say, "I Am the true Shepherd and my sheep know my voice" and will He not ascend to the throne? The living Word has a purpose for every word it speaks—to give glory to the Son of God.

We see how the living Word speaks to us, and there are many more types such as: Jacob, Adam, Samson, Solomon, Noah, Joseph, Isaac, Moses, and Boaz to name a few. There are countless shadows of events such as: the brazen serpent, water from the rock, the Ark of the Covenant, crossing the Red Sea, crossing the Jordan, and always on dry ground, for dry ground is solid ground and that is a type of resurrection ground.

The high priest entering the Holy of Holies on the Day of Atonement is a type of Christ entering the holy place in heaven after His ascension to offer the sacrifice once—for all who would believe. There are many more. Study to show yourself approved, rightly dividing the Word of truth.

Types and Shadows

We have already seen the Passover and the story of Abraham and Isaac and how they cast a shadow from some future event. How they also have a person who by their action shows a likeness to the future Jesus or a person of great importance. We will now look at the events as both shadows and types as related to the coming of the real event. We have seen that Isaac types Christ and Abraham types the Father. The ram is a type of the Lord providing Himself a sacrifice, and that sacrifice was Jesus Christ.

At the same time the wood and altar are both types and shadows of the cross. Isaac carried his own wood as Christ carried His own cross. When Moses lifted up the brazen serpent on a wood staff or pole, it was lifted up as Jesus Christ was lifted up on the cross, thus we must look up and believe.

In the record of the Passover there are types of the cross, the Lord Jesus Christ, Satan, and the rapture. There is another type and that of Egypt, as a type of the world, and we as believers must come out of the world. Therefore we see that all went out of Egypt. Everyone that did as the Lord instructed went free from bondage. Will we not think when we study *there are several million* Israelites here? Don't you think that among them there were some liars, cheaters, thieves, and a few people sleeping around if you will? There is no record that anyone who trusted the Almighty was left behind. We also who believe and trust the Lord shall come forth out of them (this world) having been redeemed of the bondage of sin.

There are types and shadows throughout the living Word of God, and when we study allowing for the Holy Ghost to reveal them to us they can be seen and understood. This is depth, it is height, it is breadth, and it is length in the Word, for it is a living Word.

Types of Israel

Within the living Word of God we continually see the use of all types of living things. We see people, such as kings, priests, farmers, ranchers, prophets, and fishermen as well as animals, fish, angels, and plant life. The fact that living things are used is simple; the book as we have seen is in fact a living thing, and all things were created by Him.

We have seen and heard the way the Word speaks to us, showing us likenesses and images of the real person and the events surrounding Him. If we will see and hear, we will see it is all speaking to our spirit of that real person, Jesus Christ, and the revelation of Him and His Word.

In every event the key people do something or represent something that the Lord Jesus Christ will later improve on, by performing the perfect work that was typed or shadowed. Let us look simply for a moment. If the sins for a year are removed from the people by an animal sacrifice and a scapegoat, what value is placed on the Creator's blood? Is it two years, fifty years, or a thousand? We should trust the Kinsman-Redeemer for it is eternity.

These important people are people that He chooses because of their faith, belief, and trust in God. As with a chessboard, He moves them at their appointed time by the foreknowledge of the Almighty. We have heard of the importance of some men and women, yet they are barely spoken of, while other names dominate the landscape of their time: each showing earthly traits and performing earthly events that will type or shadow the real event which is to come and which shall come.

When speaking of Israel God uses three living trees to represent the nation and people. The spiritual privilege symbol for Israel is the vine; the olive tree is representative of the religious privilege they held. Jesus, when referring to Israel as a nation or to their nationality, uses the fig tree.

"Yet I had planted thee a noble vine, wholly a right seed: how then art thou turned into the degenerate plant of a strange vine unto me" (Jeremiah 2:21).

He has planted the right seed, as we see through Genesis 3:15: "And I will put enmity between thee and the woman and between thy seed and her seed." At the same time He also provided Israel with a noble vine—knowledge, signs, and wonders of the one true God. But the nation turned away and rejected their King.

We must remember how God sees things: when Mary was with child, the enmity foretold by God in the garden was now placed for she was a virgin. And the Son was born of an incorruptible seed. The seed was placed in the garden and delivered through Mary at a later time, history in advance.

We know by the Word that the spiritual things of Israel are noble. But as a nation they have rejected their King; they have turned away from God to false worship and false belief, and as a nation they have denied their Messiah.

"I am the true vine, and my Father is the husbandman" (John 15:1).

Here we have our witness to the verse in Jeremiah; Christ confirms the message. He is the true vine, the Spirit of Israel, and the Father has prepared it, planted it, and provided the care of it. That true vine is the Lord Jesus Christ.

"And the trees said to the fig tree, come thou, and reign over us. But the fig tree said unto them, should I forsake my sweetness, and my good fruit, and go to be promoted over the trees?" (Judges 9:10-11).

Here we have a picture of all nations asking that Israel be promoted over all. That this has yet to happen does not change the fact that it will. We are looking into the millennial age, by history written in advance.

"Now learn the parable of the fig tree; when her branch is yet tender, and putteth forth leaves, ye know that summer is near. So ye in like manner, when ye shall see these things come to pass, know that it is nigh, even at the door" (Matthew 24:32).

Here we see the Lord Jesus Christ telling the Jews: you know how to tell summer is coming by the fig tree. Then He expects some of them to know the Scriptures (and some do), that when you see Israel bloom again, or become a nation, know that it is nigh. What is it? It is the tribulation, the great tribulation: the time of Jacob's trouble. The context is Mark 13, the signs of His coming.

The Church is never compared to a tree. As with the kingdom we see the clear difference when we compare the Church to the Jewish people and the nation of Israel. This is done by rightly dividing the Word of truth.

Therefore we can see that the Lord is giving a prophecy of May 14, 1948, when Israel is raised from the valley of dry bones. When we see Israel bloom again look up, because He is coming back. This is not to be confused with the rapture; this is the Revelation event. He is speaking to the Jew as well as to the nation of Israel. That this statement closes the prophecy is interesting because for any of it to start Israel must be in power as a nation, and May 14, 1948, solves that issue.

So we see that Jesus Christ has fulfilled His prophecy of the rebirth of Israel, and with this rebirth the signs of His coming as Israel's King of Kings and Lord of Lords would begin. Let's stop for a moment and think. To the Bride He is a Bridegroom, to the Body He is the Head, and to the Church He is our High Priest. However He is referred to as the King of the Jews. These events are related to the birth pains of a woman with child, slowly at first and gaining in rapid succession as it gets closer to the due date.

In our section on numbers we saw how they can highlight a report. From 606 BC to 1948 AD is 2,554 years; add one year for the BC/AD and you have 2,555 years. Here is the report, 2+5+5+5=17, one nation, perfectly sealed. 1+7=8, in 1948 Israel started a new beginning. Almighty God controls all times and seasons, His wonders to perform.

CHAPTER EIGHT

MYSTERIES OF HEAVEN: CODE NAME PARABLES

In these kingdom parables we are shown types and shadows of the kingdom of heaven. We are shown the coming Church and Body of the saved. We are shown types and shadows of the Lord Jesus Christ, His mission, and the work of the Holy Ghost and Father. We see and hear the truth and the purpose for parables to be used as the required method of communication by the Lord Jesus Christ.

For a very long time many pastors, preachers, and teachers have altered the root meaning of the parables, either through misunderstanding or by purpose. This is often done in support of their view, and in some cases to justify their riches. In Mark 4:13-20, for example, we find the parable of the seed. It has been misused more than any Scripture in history. It is used by all the biggies to plant money and to expect a harvest. The age old story of the hundredfold is the favorite of many who twist the Word for gain. All the while it is in fact a parable concerning the Word of God and actually bears no witness to money whatsoever.

This parable is given not to the Church but rather to the nation of Israel and concerns the truth of how they have responded to the Word of God. While it is self-evident that this is good instruction for believers, the message is nonetheless to Israel—how few would hear and truly believe. Again this speaks of our time and how many reject the gift today. But nonetheless it was spoken to Israel. They were to have been the tool used of God, but they would not and thus became blinded in part.

Let us first see the purpose for the Lord Jesus Christ to speak in parables. There are two reasons why some information given by the Word of God, Jesus Christ, was to be cloaked in parables.

"I will open my mouth in parables: I will utter dark sayings of old" (Psalm 78:2).

"That it might be fulfilled which was spoken, by the prophet, saying, I will open my mouth in parables, I will utter things which have been kept secret from the foundation of the world" (Matthew 13:35).

"And the disciples came, and said unto him, why speakest thou unto them in parables? He answered and said unto them, because it is given unto you to know the mysteries of the kingdom of heaven, but to them it is not given" (Matthew 13:10-11).

Again we need to understand what has been said here. He is disclosing secrets and mysteries, and they are cloaked in parables to confound the unbeliever and to foretell that which was to be brought to both Jew and Gentile by His vessel Paul. Let us stop here and think on some information contained in the Word. We are informed as to the Lamb's book of life in a number of references in the Bible and several contained in this study.

We all should be aware that in that book the names of the saved are written. We need to give careful consideration to this book. For we are told they were placed there before the world, before the foundations of the world. Now if that is so, it is by the supernatural foreknowledge of the Creator, for we have free will. Does it stand to reason that if your name is not already in the book either in print or some other written form, it might not be allowed in the book? For this is a completed book. Therefore we may conclude that the ones who could not see weren't supposed to see, because even seeing they would not believe.

"The secret things belong unto the LORD our God: but those things which are revealed belong unto us and our children for ever, that we may do all the words of this law" (Deuteronomy 29:29).

We now see why He spoke to the people in parables: first to fulfill the prophets, second to introduce the kingdom of heaven, not the earthly kingdom. By speaking in parables some would understand, some would not, and certainly not as a nation. Remember Israel is blinded in part. When people do not understand something what do you have? You have a secret and a mystery. Some of this information has been kept secret from the foundation of the world. As we have seen, that may have been a long, long time ago in past ages.

In the sections ahead we will see that as Paul tells us the Church was a mystery, but that it was in the foundation, and before the foundation of the world. This is later confirmed in the book of Revelation. The Word of God is a living Word. We should not seek for the dead among the living.

New Cloth on Old Garments

"And He spake also a parable unto them; No man putteth a piece of new garment upon the old; if otherwise, then both the new maketh a rent, and the piece that was taken out of the new agreeth not with the old" (Luke 5:36).

New Wine in Old Bottles

"And no man putteth new wine into old bottles, else the new wine will burst the bottles, and be spoiled, and the bottles will perish. But new wine must be put into new bottles; and both are preserved" (Luke 5:37-38).

We own a very nice suit or dress; it is the best we can afford. It gets caught on something and torn, or burnt at the cleaners. We are not going to another suit or dress and start cutting a patch out of it to fix the damage. They won't match, and the patch will destroy both. Likewise when new wine is put in old bottles, what happens? The bottles burst. But if you put new wine in new bottles they both are safe. It is so of the Spirit which does not agree with the flesh.

Therefore we see the old cloth and the old bottles are the type of the natural man, and the owner of the garment is Jesus Christ. The bottles and garment type the glorified body and the wine types the Spirit of God. He won't put the new man of the Spirit into the natural man. The natural man cannot contain the Spirit of God in its full glory, "for the natural man receives not the things of God."

This temporary house is just that, it houses the Holy Ghost on the inside—our heart not our flesh. When we are clothed in the full glory of God this decaying body of flesh and blood cannot stand, it is not suitable for that job; it must die so that we may live in the new glorified body of flesh and bone, "for this corruptible must put on incorruption and this mortal must put on immortality" (1 Corinthians 15:53).

We know from the conversation on the mountain that Moses could not look upon God and live. He was placed in a cleft in the rock and saw His backside. Now this is prevalent within the Word of God. Prophet after prophet cannot stand when visited by an angel or type of the glorified Christ, not the real thing. It is your spirit and soul that puts on immortality, as one would put on a coat. The blood of our Kinsman-Redeemer is how our new coat is provided, and at some point we all will have the new coat put on us. As always He will put it on us just as He did with Adam and Eve.

The Hidden Treasure

"Again, the kingdom of heaven is like unto treasure hid in a field; the which when a man hath found, he hideth, and for joy thereof goeth and selleth all that he hath, and buyeth that field" (Matthew 13:44).

The Pearl of Great Price

"And again the kingdom of heaven is like unto a merchant man, seeking goodly pearls, who when he had found one pearl of great price, went and sold all that he had and bought it" (Matthew 13:45-46).

Many people misunderstand the parable of the pearl of great price. One Christian radio host explained that the Church is the merchant man, and the pearl is Jesus Christ. This simply cannot be for if the grace of God is a gift, then what do we sell to receive it? One does not buy a gift, one receives a gift. We, the one Bride, Body, and Church, do not nor have we ever sold all that we have to receive our salvation. We are as Rebekah, who was adorned before she ever met her bridegroom. Again the Church is never compared to a man, for it is one Body made up of many. In Paul's letter to the Ephesians he explains this as follows:

"In whom ye also trusted, after that ye heard the word of truth, the gospel of your salvation: in whom also after that ye believe, ye were sealed with that Holy Spirit of promise. Which is the earnest of our inheritance until the redemption of the purchased possession, unto the praise of his glory" (Ephesians 1:13-14).

When our trust is in the finished works of our Kinsman-Redeemer, Jesus Christ, through our faith we then receive the gospel of salvation. It is sealed by the indwelling of the Holy Spirit. It is earnest of our inheritance, a deposit if you will. "Until the redemption of the purchased possession." Or you might say until the closing date, when all debts are settled.

If we are in the market for some farmland and in our pursuit of it we find some land with gold deposits and no one else is aware of this fact, would we not sell all we had to buy that farm? Of course we would. And if we're shopping and we find a pearl of great value, we can greatly increase our wealth! Would we not sell all that we had to buy the pearl? Of course we would.

The Lord Jesus Christ Himself is the buyer and the merchant; He is buying a Church. He gave up all that He had to purchase the field and the pearl. We are the field and the pearl. We: the field as many members make one Body and that one Body makes a Bride, and the Bride is the pearl, His Church. Through leaving the heavens and giving up all that He had, He goes to the cross to provide the blood sacrifice that is the price of the field and the pearl.

"For ye know the grace of our Lord Jesus Christ, that, though he were rich, yet for your sakes he became poor, that ye through his poverty might be rich" (2 Corinthians 8:9).

Again, we who are the people for His name, we are the field, and as the Word discloses we have been hidden. Together we make up one Body, the Church, and that is the pearl. He willingly gave up all that He had. So the many false teachers that will preach to us how Jesus was rich and owned houses and designer clothes—by the Word of God this is either a lie or a serious misunderstanding. Poverty does not mean rich and poor does not equate to wealth. So such is the truth of our Redeemer that He gave up all He had to gain the more.

We clearly see and hear, and thus understand, that the one who gave up all that He had was not the Church but rather the Lord Himself, the Son of the Most High, Jesus Christ. He left His first estate; He gave it up to gain the more—His Body, His Church, and His Bride. We have not defeated Satan, He hath defeated Satan. It has been accounted to us. This is the power of God, and this is to His glory, to all who will believe on Him.

The Net

"Again the kingdom of heaven is like unto a net that was cast into the sea, and gathered of every kind: which, when it was full, they drew to shore, and sat down, and gathered the good into vessels, but cast the bad away. So shall it be at the end of the world: the angels shall come forth, and sever the wicked from among the just, and shall cast them into the furnace of fire: there shall be wailing and gnashing of teeth" (Matthew 13:47-50).

As we have seen mistakes are made when these parables are applied to money, riches, and worldly things. We also see how misunderstanding can alter the true meaning of the Word. We should understand from the field as well as the pearl what the living Word says.

Here we see in the parable of the net what the living Word speaks to us of the kingdom of heaven. That He says "like unto" types the parable. The net is the Holy Ghost, the sea is humanity, and we certainly are a diverse group are we not? When the net was full (fullness of the Gentiles) it was pulled ashore and then they gave the good into vessels (we get a new body), and so the vessel is a type of the resurrected body.

Within this parable is also a gap. When the angels come we have moved into the seventieth week of Daniel; these are those saved out of the great tribulation. The bad, a type of unbelievers, are cast away. The fact that angels come to separate the two shows us it is not the Church. The bad go to a furnace of fire. This sounds a lot like judgment to me.

In these parables we are a field, a sea, a pearl, clothing, fish of every kind, and we do very little if anything to get what we receive: a new glorious and everlasting home, and a new and perfect body, purchased and kept by the grace of God by faith in the finished works of our Kinsman-Redeemer, Jesus Christ.

The Two Debtors

"There was a certain creditor which had two debtors: the one owed five hundred pence, and the other fifty. And when they had nothing to pay, he frankly forgave them both. Tell me therefore, which of them will love him the most. Simon answered and said, I suppose that he, to whom he forgave the most. And he said unto him thou hast rightly judged" (Luke 7:41-43).

Here we see the creditor is God, and the two are debtors, and frankly He just said forget about it. In other words He cancelled or pardoned the debt. The lesson here is that both were forgiven. The Lord wants us to see and hear as we are given a very profound lesson; which of the two loved Him the most? Is it not the one who was forgiven the most?

Here we have a side lesson. There was one coming born out of due time, and he would outwork all the others. He was forgiven much and was shown the hidden secrets of the grace of God, the apostle Paul.

The Lost Coin

"Either what woman having ten pieces of silver, if she lose one piece, doth not light a candle, and sweep the house, and seek diligently till she find it. And when she hath found it, she calleth her friends and neighbors together, saying, Rejoice with me; for I have found the piece that I had lost. Likewise, I say unto you, there is joy in the presence of the angels of God over one sinner that repenteth" (Luke 15:8-10).

Here we are compared to a piece of silver. The woman who lost it turns on a light, and when men see that light and go to it, that light is Jesus Christ. The lost is found and restored to her. And when man repents and calls to the finished works of Jesus Christ, he builds on that foundation which is Solid Rock. Therein lies the power unto salvation. Therefore the angels sing to God over the joy of each one of us who yields to the voice of the Shepherd, the Light of the World, Jesus Christ.

The Pharisee and the Publican

In Luke 18:9-14 we hear the parable of the Pharisee and those who justify themselves. Jesus sets the stage for the parable with the self-righteous man and the sinner. One offers a prayer of self and one of mercy. Let's read the account.

"And he spake this parable unto certain which trusted in themselves that they were righteous, and despised others: Two men went up into the temple to pray; the one a Pharisee the other a publican. The Pharisee stood and prayed this with himself, God I thank thee that I am not as other men are, extortioners, unjust, adulterers, or even as this publican. I fast twice a week and pay tithes of all that I possess. And the publican standing afar off would not so much as lift up his eyes unto heaven, but smote upon his breast, saying, God be merciful to me a sinner. I tell you, this man went down to his house justified rather than the other: for everyone that exalteth himself shall be abased; and he that humbleth himself shall be exalted" (Luke 18:9-14).

First let's look at the prophecy, "the humble would be exalted." What did our dear Savior do? He gave all glory unto the Father, humbled Himself, and went to the cross. And He arose after three days and nights; thus He was exalted. He is fulfilling His own prophecy and giving us a view of what it means to deny oneself and call out to God for the salvation that is in Christ Jesus.

The prayer of the sinner was based on humility and belief. He believed that if God would, He could save him. The prayer of the self-righteous man was to himself, thanking God for his greatness and boasting of his works. We see whom God justifies; it is the one who humbled himself, the sinner! We also know by history and faith that the Lord Jesus Christ took on our sin, and the one who bore our sin went to His house justified. And as the result we are justified through and by our Lord Jesus Christ. It might be safe to add here that it is extremely difficult to find a humble TV preacher these days; for the most part they seem to all glory in and of themselves.

Remember the five hundred pence and the fifty pence. Both are using the number five; it is by grace they were pardoned of the debt. Even though it took ten times more grace for the one, it seems there was enough for both. Now we have the rest of the story.

Very seldom do we read of these parables as being prophecy when in fact they are. They are both types and shadows of future events and they provide for us a completely different set of facts when the living Word is rightly divided.

The living Word is not a motivational book, and it is not a name-it-claim-it book. It certainly contains both motivation and blessing; however it is the revelation of God. It is the living Word of God Almighty. It tells of a Prince, a King, a Kinsman-Redeemer, a Mighty Warrior, a Judge, a Creator, a Provider, a Protector, a Chastiser, a Brazen Serpent, the Ancient of Days, a Passover Lamb, and a Bright and Morning Star. It is the revelation of the Lord Jesus Christ, the glory of God.

The living Word of God shows His love, His anger, His power, His mercy, His judgment, and His grace, and all unlimited. It is alive because the author still lives. The Word is still unfolding on the world stage. If we are unable to admit such, then may God open our eyes and bless us with understanding, for verily I say, beloved, time is indeed short.

His love for us is never ending; it will never stop. His mercy is unconditional when our faith is in His finished work. Therefore His grace is enough. It should be by this knowledge that we live a victorious life and not by the riches of this world.

Let me be clear here. I do not dislike money; fill my pocket, Lord. It is not the amount of money but rather the manner by which it is obtained, and to what end it is promised to be used, and how it is then used. Teachers should be paid and paid well, but $9,000 for a one-night layover, arriving in your private jet, and riding in your limousine may be a bit much. All the while many people have no place to lay their head. This includes the Lord, who had no place to lay His head. Come on, man!

CHAPTER NINE

MYSTERIES OF GOD: CODE NAME PAUL'S GOSPEL

Paul was an amazing man, and God called him to disclose the mystery and secrets of the Church and the truth of the gospel. Paul was a Pharisee among Pharisees, a Jew of very high rank. He was also a Roman citizen, highly educated in Jewish law and tradition. He was given the authority and the papers to waste the Church. He was provided the means and support to travel far and wide in pursuit of "believers" to kill, torture, and otherwise destroy the Church. He was a bounty hunter's bounty hunter if you will.

Paul was present at the stoning of Stephen and even held the coats of those who stoned him, showing his authority. He was zealous in his pursuit of the destruction of the Body of Christ. But the Lord blinded him, spoke to him, and showed him things that no other prophet had ever understood—the secrets and mysteries of the ages.

"Now to Him that is of power to stablish you according to my gospel, and the preaching of Jesus Christ, according to the revelation of the mystery, which was kept secret since the world began" (Romans 16:25).

While the Church was never in the Old Testament it is both typed and shadowed in the Old Testament. That the prophets could not understand the dispensation of grace by faith, and the fullness of the Gentiles, is because they were not allowed to see the gap between the cross and the crown: the dispensation of grace by faith.

We know this is so because Paul uses these types and shadows more than any other apostle; he was well educated in all things Jewish and all things Israel. Paul as a Roman citizen was free to go anywhere in the Roman Empire. Paul covered more miles, taught more people, and established more churches than did all the others, and they were all over the known world.

There are records of visits to Spain, France, and England, proclaiming the gospel, his gospel. He taught in Greece, Turkey, Rome, and throughout the known world. Paul's message by revelation was one of grace by faith, through the shed blood of Jesus on the cross and His glorious resurrection, His ascending, and the acceptance of the sacrifice by the Father; that He did enter once into the Holy of Holies, thereby overcoming death, hell, and the grave. Jesus had defeated sin, He had overcome the world

Paul was an amazing speaker and writer. In his letters he speaks and writes like a lawyer. He will explain, explain, and explain and then close with a factual statement and the disclosing of Scripture to support the truth shown to him. God had chosen the one to whom the mystery was proclaimed and He had chosen well.

We must understand, and may I say be thankful, that God does not need a bunch of old guys in robes to vote on who He speaks to; He needs no Mullah [??] or a bunch of TV preachers, deacons, elders, or any of us for that matter. It is said "my sheep hear my voice and follow." He can speak to anyone He chooses and by any means He wants. He even spoke once though a donkey. It is also written in the living

Word of God "in these last days He has spoken to us by His Son." We can see that He is perfectly suited for the job.

The Gospel of the Blood

"Take heed therefore unto yourselves, and to all the flock, over which the Holy Ghost hath made you overseers, to feed the church of God which he hath purchased with his own blood" (Acts 20:28).

"Being justified freely by his grace through the redemption that is in Christ Jesus: whom God hath set forth to be a propitiation through faith in his blood, to declare his righteousness for the remission of sins that are past. Through the forbearance of God; to declare I say, at this time his righteousness: that he might be just, and the justifier of them that believeth in Jesus. Where is boasting then? It is excluded. By what law? Of works? Nay: but by the law of faith. Therefore we conclude that a man is justified by faith without the deeds of the law" (Romans 3:24-28).

"Much more than being now justified by his blood, we shall be saved from wrath through him. For if, when we were enemies, we were reconciled to God by the death of his Son, much more, being reconciled, we shall be saved by his life and not only so, but we also joy in God through our Lord Jesus Christ, by whom we have received the atonement" (Romans 5:9-11).

"In whom we have redemption through his blood, the forgiveness of sins, according to the riches of his grace; wherein he hath abounded to us in all wisdom and prudence; having made known to us the mystery of his will, according to his good pleasure which he hath purposed in himself: that in the dispensation of the fullness of times he might gather together all things in Christ, both which are in heaven and which are on the earth; even in him: in whom also we have obtained an inheritance, being predestinated according to the purpose of him who worketh all things after the counsel of his own will: that we should be the praise of his glory, who first trusted in Christ" (Ephesians 1:7-12).

We should be amazed when we see how the Word is alive; how when we read from different books and letters and different locations, it reads as if it were written as one thought. Why? This is because there may be several scribes, but only one author. The Word of God must be studied and rightly divided, and when it is it comes to life; it is the living Word of God, just waiting on us to receive its revelation and understanding.

We see here the authority is the Holy Ghost. He is giving instructions to feed the Church, for a great price was paid to obtain it: His own blood. He goes on to say He is who hath made us just. How? He did it by Himself through the blood of the Lamb, Jesus Christ. Therefore it is believing this fact that becomes the "law of faith."

Hear the living Word proclaim faith is a law! If a law, it is in Christ and Christ fulfilled the law. If a law, it is of the cross and the shed blood. If a law, then that of resurrection and the ascending! If a law, then that of the ransom and redemption. Therefore we may declare: past is gone and we are now declared by forbearance to be seen as righteous always.

We are told that by His blood we are not only justified but saved from wrath. Is not the great tribulation called the wrath of God? Is not the time of Jacob's trouble the time of great tribulation and therefore the wrath of God? There goes that no-rapture thing again.

We joy in Christ for He hath provided atonement, not just *an* atonement but *the* atonement. Our Kinsman-Redeemer did this on our behalf. He died in our place. We should read the story of Barabbas and Christ; a guilty man goes free and an innocent man dies in his place (Matthew 27:16-26).

Then we hear that during the dispensation of the fullness of time He is gathering all things in heaven and earth to Himself. We have been purchased; no option is on us but rather a deed. Are we not called His Body? The Kinsman-Redeemer hath prevailed to pay the price with His blood. Jesus Christ restores us to our inheritance. Why? We are His glory. Why? We trust Him, by faith, because He lives!

Before we proceed to Paul's gospel of the cross let us review some facts. Provided for us from the book of Acts, Romans, and Ephesians are fourteen verses rightly divided, providing fourteen works of His blood. This was the purchase price for the right to negotiate with us. It was not gold or silver but rather a perfect life and the blood thereof. The Kinsman-Redeemer paid for us, and here are some of the terms He offers in His contract.

He hath purchased, He hath justified, He hath called us righteous, He hath fulfilled the law of faith, He hath saved us from wrath, He hath provided redemption, He hath provided riches by His grace, He hath purposed this in Himself, He hath provided an inheritance, He hath predestinated us, He hath given us wisdom, He hath reconciled us, He hath become the atonement, He hath made us the praise of His glory. Contained here in the report is the witness (1+4=5). The number of grace coincides with both the number of verses and the number of works He provided for us. Please, someone tell us if they can: what is left for us to do? But only we shall put our faith in Jesus Christ and His finished works.

The Gospel of the Cross

"For Christ sent me not to baptize, but to preach the gospel: not with wisdom of words, lest the cross of Christ be made of none effect, for the teaching of the cross is to them that perish foolishness; but unto us that are saved it is the power of God. For it is written, I will destroy the wisdom of the wise, and will bring to nothing the understanding of the prudent" (1 Corinthians 1:17-19).

"But God forbid that I should glory, save in the cross of our Lord Jesus Christ, by whom the world is crucified unto me, and I unto the world. For in Christ Jesus neither circumcision availeth anything nor uncircumcision, but a new creature" (Galatians 6:14-15).

"And having made peace through the blood of his cross, by him to reconcile all things to himself; by him, I say, whether they be things in earth, or things in heaven" (Colossians 1:20).

Paul's gospel once again declares to us that we are saved by faith through the finished works of Jesus Christ, and that the cross is the focal point. He is the one who has reconciled all things to Himself, by Himself. Not by men who claim to live a holy life or tell us such foolishness. While all who believe in the power of God through Christ Jesus should live for Him, the truth is we can't cut it in this flesh. For by the Word He proclaims, "your righteousness is as filthy rags" (Isaiah 64:6).

"Looking unto Jesus the author and finisher of our faith; who for the joy that was set before him endured the cross, despising the shame, and is set down at the right hand of the throne of God" (Hebrews 12:2).

Once again these verses just flow together and come alive when they are read from the living Word of God, rightly divided. Then light is shone on us that we may see. Paul is quick to let us know it is not by baptizing but by the teaching of the cross which, while foolish to the natural man, to the spirit man is the power of God unto salvation.

Paul explains he is dead to the world and the world is dead to him, therefore we also are dead to the world and the world is dead to us. He is a new creature born again of the spirit man, and that same hope of glory lives in us. It is the spirit that will be saved not our flesh, and that by the cross and blood payment of the Lamb of God, Jesus Christ. For the Word proclaims for all to hear: "God sees those things which be not, as though they already were." Paul preaches, writes, and works on this belief, revealed by the Holy Ghost, that we are already seated in heavenly places.

Before we proceed to Paul's gospel of grace by faith let us review the cross. The old wooden cross takes the place of the altar and thereby becomes the altar. It is the tool used to perform the work. By the cross God through Jesus Christ supplies a list of accomplished work.

Once more the agreement is expanded. By the cross comes reconciliation, the power of God unto salvation; by the cross He made peace; by the cross the world is crucified; by the cross we are a new creation; and by the cross seated with Christ on the right hand of authority.

The Gospel of Grace by Faith

"And declared to be the Son of God with power, according to the spirit of holiness, by the resurrection of the dead: by whom we have received grace and apostleship, for obedience to the faith among all nations, for his name: Among whom are thee also the called of Jesus Christ" (Romans 1:4-6).

"Therefore being justified by faith we have peace with God through our Lord Jesus Christ. By whom we have access by faith unto this grace wherein we stand, and rejoice in hope of the glory of God" (Romans 1:1-2).

"For by grace are ye saved through faith; and that not of yourselves it is a free gift of God: not of works, lest any man should boast" (Eph. 2:8-9).

"Now our Lord Jesus Christ Himself and God even our Father, which hath loved us, and hath given us everlasting consolation and good hope through grace" (2 Thessalonians 2:16).

"The grace of our Lord Jesus Christ be with your spirit. Amen" (Philemon 25).

The living Word of God is really a marvelous thing to behold. How the living Word fits together like a perfectly constructed building, the perfection with which the Holy Ghost is always in harmony—it is a marvelous thing to behold. The detail provided is always a witness, and there always is a witness through Scripture, through numbers, or through history itself.

We hear the Holy Ghost declare Jesus the Son of God. He rose from the dead and He is alive! He has provided grace for us by our faith, and for His name we are called. Our peace with God is through Him: the finished works of Jesus Christ. It is then by faith that we receive grace, a gift of God, and the power thereof. No boasting is allowed. This truly hurts the self-proclaimed perfectionist, or those who claim a sinless life. There are few things within the Church as disgusting as self-righteousness.

While we have a standing with the Father through the work of the Son, there is nothing we can boast about. In fact it is He who loved us and hath given us everlasting consolation and good hope through faith. Not to our natural man, but rather our born-again spirit, our new creation.

One of the hardest things for us as believers is to understand the two creations. We are of the natural, earthy. We are also of the spirit, heavenly. The living Word of God clearly speaks to both. We must learn, by the Word and the Spirit, to separate the two. Paul is very clear, when rightly divided, to whom grace is given. There are few if any gray areas with Paul. Trust God and His Word. You have no need that any man teach you but rather the Holy Ghost. We who are called to preach and teach are tutors more than teachers; it is through the desire of knowing Him that we will learn.

Many fight against the truth for they would rather believe a lie. There hath been one perfect man, a 100 percent man, and 100 percent perfect. There is one perfect Son of God, 100 percent perfect and 100 percent God! To assume that mankind can please Almighty God with the works of our hands is to be as Cain: foolish. Our mistakes, sins, and thoughts are simply contrary to the Word of God. To assume anyone can elevate their life to His acceptance through works is utterly foolish and self-righteous. They deny the immeasurable love of God; they deny the true power of God. For is it not written, He will give mercy and grace to whom He will? Do we live like the devil? No we do not. However it is by grace that we do our best to please God and to show our gratitude for our salvation. While the right works may earn us reward, they unfortunately will not earn us salvation.

The Gospel of the Resurrection

"Jesus said unto her, I am the resurrection and the life: he that believeth in me, though he were dead, yet shall he live: and whosoever liveth and believeth in me shall never die, believeth thou this?" (John 11:25-26).

"And have hope toward God, which they themselves also allow, that there shall be a resurrection of the dead, both of the just and the unjust" (Acts 24:15).

"Now if Christ be preached that he rose from the dead, how say some among you that there is no resurrection of the dead? But if there be no resurrection, then is Christ not risen, and if Christ be not risen, then is our preaching vain, and your faith is also vain" (1 Corinthians 15:12-14).

"That I may know him and the power of his resurrection, and the fellowship of his sufferings, being made conformable to his death; if by any means I might attain unto the resurrection of the dead" (Philippians 3:10-11).

"By faith Abraham when he was tried, offered up Isaac: and he that had received the promise offered up his only begotten son, of whom it was said, that in Isaac shall thy seed be called: according that God was able to raise him up, even from the dead: from whence also he received him in a figure" (Hebrews 11:17-19).

    The Lord Jesus Christ is the resurrection and the life, and we are told this: that being dead we live, and living and believing we will never die. Will we believe this?
    Once again we clearly see the rapture, from the words of the Bridegroom Jesus Christ. It is as if He is saying: if you are alive when I call, you will never die. In this we place our trust that we have hope toward God. That the complete harmony of Father, Son, and Holy Ghost provide that we can have this hope.
    Paul tells us there will be a resurrection of both the saved and the unsaved. Therefore, because He has risen from the dead, we should not question our own; because if He did not rise, then our hope and our faith is wasted and of no value.

But the Spirit and the Word bear witness that He is raised and that He was, is, and forever will be.

We then hear that we are made conformable to His death and sufferings. By this we can look to our resurrection, for we are counted as dead already in Christ, yea even more counted as alive in Him. We should be always mindful that God sees those things that are not as though they were.

Remember Abraham and Isaac; for Abraham believed and trusted God. He believed that if he were to slay Isaac, God would raise him up again from the dead. Therefore we know that Abraham had faith in resurrection power for he said "the lad and I will return." For as the True and Faithful Witness, Jesus Christ, told them, "destroy this temple and I will raise it up again in three days." They were thinking as the natural man; they looked at the building not knowing the Scriptures—that God was in Christ and Christ in God. They are one.

We know by the Word that all power has been given Him; so in life, in death, and in resurrection they are all in His power. Everything created was by His power, His wisdom, and His direction. All things were made by Him, through Him, of Him, for Him, and in Him. Resurrection is the power of God that rewards salvation, through grace by faith. Therefore, beloved, we put our faith in "the finished works of Jesus Christ."

We often wonder how is it that we will be changed, for our soul and spirit are already so; they are seen as a citizen seated in heavenly places. We shall be clothed with an incorruptible body, fashioned as the Lord when He arose from the dead and walked with the two on the road and broke bread and was gone, appearing in the upper room.

"For our conversation is in heaven, from whence we also look to the Savior, the Lord Jesus Christ. Who shall change our vile body, that it may be fashioned to his glorious body, according to the working whereby he is able even to subdue all things unto himself" (Philippians 3:20-21).

The Mystery of the Church

"And I say unto thee, that thou art Peter, and upon this rock I will build my church, and the gates of hell shall not prevail against it" (Matthew 16:18).

"And he answered and said unto them, because it is given unto you to know the mysteries of the kingdom of heaven, but to them it is not given" (Matthew 13:11).

"And when they had come to Jerusalem, they were received of the church, and of the apostles and elders, and they declared all things that God had done with them" (Acts 15:4).

"But we speak the wisdom of God in a mystery, even the hidden wisdom, which God ordained before the world unto our glory" (1 Corinthians 2:7).

"For the husband is the head of his wife, even as Christ is the head of the church: and he is the saviour of the body" (Ephesians 5:23).

"Let no man so account of us, as of the ministers of Christ, and the stewards of the mysteries of God" (1 Corinthians 4:1).

"To the general assembly and church of the first born, which are written in heaven and to God the judge of all, and to the spirits of just men made perfect" (Hebrews 12:23).

"And to make all men see what is the fellowship of the mystery, which from the beginning of the world hath been hid in God, who created all things by Jesus Christ" (Ephesians 3:9).

"And for me, that utterance may be given unto me, that I may open my mouth boldly, to make known the mystery of the gospel" (Ephesians 6:19).

"Holding the mystery of the faith in a pure conscience" (1 Timothy 3:9).

Frodo can have the fellowship of the ring. I'll take the fellowship of the mystery. Once again we see with clarity when the Word is rightly divided and linked together. We are told that the Church, the gospel, and even our faith are a mystery. We are introduced to this by Jesus Christ. Paul expounds on the subject. Why? Because to Paul was the stewardship of the mystery given.

To Paul was it disclosed that the Church was in God before the foundations of the world—that's a long time. In the Old Testament faith was belief. God spoke to people directly and through prophets. In the New Testament belief is faith. How much we have and in whom we put it is the question.

We've never moved a mountain. But we have seen healing miracles and lives changed. We have felt the Spirit move. We have seen Him in our life, time and time again. He stands at the doorway of our heart knocking that He may enter in and give us rest. We are most assuredly told by Paul it is the spirit of just men made perfect, and by whom it is made thus and so.

What kind of church are we, Methodist, Baptist, Episcopal, Catholic? No, we are the Church of the First Born, Jesus Christ. It is in this fellowship that we are part of the fellowship, as in the fellowship of the Church if you will. This fellowship was purchased at a high price. We have been hidden in God from before He created the world; it is the power unto salvation, and the power of God unto resurrection.

It has been His good pleasure that by one man's life He brings life, for in one man's fall all were condemned. By the disobedience of the first Adam was sin and the wages of sin, which is death, given to man.

Then by the obedient life of the second Adam will many receive life. It is not so much that the Old Testament prophets did not see and hear, but rather understand. It was hidden, as to the manner that God had prepared our salvation through Jesus Christ. The Church, the Body, and the Bride: that is the mystery. Paul was the one to receive. The gospel is made clear when we study, rightly dividing the Word of truth.

Let us look at two last important issues here, one concerning the Savior of the Body. Do not be confused; it is not your natural body Paul is speaking of but rather His Body, the Church. Read the Lord's words carefully for we are clearly told in Matthew 16:18 "will build my Church." Therefore it is clear both in history and the living Word that at that moment it was yet to be built. The rock is not Peter it is the Word that Peter spoke and believed that the Church will be built upon; Jesus is the Solid Rock, and only by revelation can we proclaim it so.

The Gospel of Judgment

"In the days when God shall judge the secrets of men by Jesus Christ according to my gospel" (Romans 2:16).

This one doesn't need much explaining but rather some insight from the Holy Ghost. We have read in this section about the gospel of Paul, that there is no place in Paul's message for self. It gives us nothing to add to that which is done by God through Jesus Christ and the witness thereof by the

Holy Ghost; for it is the perfect work that the Kinsman our Lord hath performed.

Paul is making known the fact that it will be by his gospel, not Matthew, Mark, Luke, or John. Not Peter, not David or Moses, and not any other, but that Jesus Christ will judge all men by Paul's gospel. Therefore contained in the works of Paul, all fourteen books, is the message that will make up the gospel to the Church, and how all are judged. Our salvation is in the hands of God, because we are the Body, and in Christ and Christ in us, and Christ is in God and God is in Christ. The fact that we are not yet there does not change the fact that we are seen as one with the Father. Does not God see those things which be not as though they were?

We also know that the wages of sin is death. So payment for sin is death. None of us in this body live forever, we all die. We would therefore say that there has been no man or woman who ever overcame sin by works of the flesh. But be of good cheer, for the Lamb of God hath overcome the world, and when we trust in His finished works, so have we!

Within the book of Zechariah God allows the prophet to see an event unfold which will be explained by the apostle Paul hundreds of years later. As with Peleg, God will fill in the blanks at a different time, according to His purpose. In this account a high priest, Joshua, is standing before the LORD with Satan on his right side, the side of authority. Satan's purpose at this meeting is clear; Satan is the accuser of the brethren. Also present at this event was an angel of the Lord, a personal assistant if you will. In the account of the event we are given a type and shadow of justification through Christ Jesus.

Even as Joshua stands before God with filthy clothes, typing the works of his flesh, the works of his hands, Satan doesn't even get to slander him before Almighty God speaks: clean him, put fine clothes on him, and place a crown upon his head. It is clear that throughout the event all Joshua does is stand there as Satan is rebuked by the Word of God. Joshua has done nothing except show up dirty and become clothed in fine linen and gold; the Almighty hath performed all the work.

"And he showed me Joshua the high priest standing before the angel of the LORD, and Satan standing on his right hand to resist him. And the angel of the LORD spake unto Satan, the LORD rebuke thee. O Satan, even the LORD that hath chosen Jerusalem rebuke thee: is not this a brand plucked out of the fire? Now Joshua was clothed with filthy garments, and stood before the angel. And he answered and spake unto those who stood before him. Take away the filthy garments from him. And unto him he said, Behold, I have caused thine iniquity to pass from thee, and I will clothe thee with change of raiment. And I said, Let them set a fair miter upon his head. So they set a fair miter upon his head, and clothed him with garments. And the angel of the LORD stood by" (Zechariah 3:1-5).

Paul is shown the details pertaining to the eternal secrets of God. Paul explains why it is by faith and not by works. What on earth did Joshua do on his own behalf? Nothing: in the flesh he was dirty, unclean, and sinful. He offered no defense for his condition. However he had been branded in the fire, he had kept the faith. And so the Lamb slain before the foundation, the Kinsman-Redeemer, respecter of no persons, hath declared him right before God.

So by faith in the finished works of Jesus Christ we are saved, and without that faith we are not saved. Both the just and unjust will be judged, one by grace and one by justice. For all have missed the mark; "for without faith it is impossible to please God" (Hebrews 11:6).

CHAPTER TEN

JESUS: CODE NAME KINSMAN-REDEEMER

The living Word of God proclaims Jesus Christ from the beginning until the end. The Bible contains the message of His power, His glory, His love, His passion, and yes His anger and wrath. It reveals His current work, His past work, and yes His future work. We will look at them through the Scripture and information provided in relationship to His majesty, His atonement, and His ownership of the power of salvation and resurrection.

Alpha and Omega

"I Am the Alpha and Omega, the Beginning and the Ending, saith the Lord which is, and which was and is to come, the Almighty" (Revelation 1:8).

"Saying I Am the Alpha and Omega the First and Last: and what thou seest, write in a book and send to the seven churches which are in Asia" (Revelation 1:11).

"And unto the angel of the church of the Laodiceans write; these things saith the Amen, the Faithful and True Witness, the Beginning of the Creation of God" (Revelation 3:14).

"I am the Alpha and Omega, the Beginning and the End, the First and Last" (Revelation 22:13).

Can you imagine such a thing? I think not, at least not by the natural man, but by the Spirit we have wisdom. We know that He is much more than First and Last, but also all things in between. Here He uses several of His names: Lord, Alpha and Omega, Beginning and Ending, First and Last, I Am, Faithful Witness, Beginning of Creation, Amen and Almighty. Nine names are used; therefore we see the stamp of the fullness of blessing put on the information provided through the living Word of God. It should be possible for us to realize that in the millennium and ages to follow we will most certainly live in the fullness of blessing. He has always been, He will always be, and He is coming soon. He stands at the beginning of time and the end of time at the same time. He is God, "and there is none other" (Isaiah 45:5).

The Broken Body

"But he was wounded for our transgressions, he was bruised for our iniquities; the chastisement of our peace was upon him; and with his stripes we are healed" (Isaiah 53:5).

"And he took bread, and gave thanks, and brake it, and gave unto them, saying. This is my body which is given for you, this do in remembrance of me" (Luke 22:19).

"And when he had given thanks, he brake it, and said, take, eat: this is my body, which is broken for you, this do in remembrance of me" (1 Corinthians 11:24).

We see that He did much more for us than forgive our sin, He hath also healed us. The beating that He took was for our peace and the lashes He received were for our healing. While we have all seen or heard of many earthly healings in our years, we have also seen sickness and strife that was not healed on this earth. However, according to the Word of God, when it is provided it is not for sale or for show, but rather is a gift of God to bring forth His glory and not the glory of men and women. But let us not be ignorant of truth; there is no sickness and death in heaven. This old natural earthy man must die, but we are seen as healed and healed forever through Jesus Christ.

When we come to the table of the Lord, we do not come to eat His flesh, we come to break the bread and He is the Bread of Life. We are to do this in remembrance of Him and the price He paid on our behalf, for the love He hath shown to us cannot be measured.

The Blood of the Lamb

"For this is my blood of the New Testament, which is shed for many for the remission of sins" (Matthew 26:28).

"And in the same manner also he took the cup, when he had supped, saying; this cup is the New Testament in my blood: this do ye, as often as you drink it, in remembrance of me" (1 Corinthians 11:25).

"Much more then, being now justified by his blood, we shall be saved from wrath through him" (Romans 5:9).

"In whom we have redemption through his blood, the forgiveness of sins, according to the riches of his grace" (Ephesians 1:7).

The New Testament is also a new covenant; it does not cancel the covenants with Israel nor replace them. It is a covenant with a new people, both Jew and Gentile called out for His name, purchased by the blood of the Lamb of God, Jesus Christ, for the forgiveness of our sin.

We are to remember Him through the Table of the Lord, and when we come to the table we must discern why we come: that He provided for us through His blood, our salvation. His love for us knows no bounds and has no end. We should also draw nigh to these words "for many," for they are not for all. While our Father through Christ Jesus wishes none to be lost, not one, this does not alter the fact that far more are lost than are found. We must trust God, for all men have heard the Word. However sad it may be, not all men will believe.

When we consider and contemplate His love, we allow our spirit to listen and draw close. We will hear of Abel, Enoch, Noah, Abraham, Isaac, Jacob, and Joseph. Of Moses, David, Solomon, and Elijah. We see the Day of Atonement, the altar and the Mercy Seat; they all speak of Jesus Christ and His finished works. All speak to us of faith, belief, grace, and the blood atoning. But here, the Creator of all—all that was, is, and will be—by the power of Himself He provides the fulfillment to all the types and shadows and pays the ransom for all the sins of those who trust in Him.

That He who created us would willingly, in humility, give His body and His life for mankind. To be subject as a servant to that which you created—no man knows such love as this. And to prove His power over all things: He was resurrected.

"For God so loved the world that he gave his only begotten Son that whosoever believeth in him should not perish, but have everlasting life" (John 3:16).

Let us understand what is not said here; it is not said who believes and lives without sin, or who believes and lives perfectly. It is not said who believes and never sins again. God simply said "whosoever believes"; there seems to be no other requirement, and by believing through faith we have everlasting life, by believing in the finished works of Jesus Christ.

The Resurrection

"The same day came unto him the Sadducees, which say that there is no resurrection, and asked him..." (Matthew 22:23).

"Jesus answered and said unto them, ye do err, not knowing the scriptures, nor the power of God" (Matthew 22:29).

"And thou shalt be blessed; for they cannot recompense thee: for thou shalt be recompensed at the resurrection of the just" (Luke 14:14).

"Jesus said unto her, I am the resurrection, and the life: he that believeth in me, though he were dead, yet shall he live" (John 11:25).

"But if there be no resurrection of the dead, then is Christ not risen" (1 Corinthians 15:13).

"That I may know him, and the power of his resurrection, and the fellowship of his sufferings, being made conformable unto his death" (Philippians 3:10).

"Blessed be the God and Father of our Lord Jesus Christ, which according to his abundant mercy has begotten us again unto a lively hope by the resurrection of Jesus Christ from the dead" (1 Peter 1:3).

We should give pause and wonder when we hear the truth how all these people of His time of visit were so deaf and blind. The Creator is walking among them. The blind can see, the deaf can hear, the dumb can speak, and the lame can walk. Lepers are healed, demons are cast out, and dead people are reinstated. How could anyone not have seen, except through the will of God? By foreknowledge that it should come to all mankind by faith, in the finished works of Jesus Christ, how is it that some will not hear?

We all see, when we look, all the false doctrines of the day: Adam was God manifested in the flesh, we are gods, you can be rich, and Jesus never claimed to be God. Israel was never offered the kingdom, Jesus never claimed to be the Messiah, or the Church has replaced Israel. The foolishness of those who teach that Adam breathed life into the animals and that God is a failure. Be ever watchful for there are many who will say anything for money and lots of it. There are many wolves in the clothing of sheep.

"For we are not as many, who corrupt the word of God: but as of sincerity, but as of God, in the sight of God speak we of Christ" (2 Corinthians 2:17).

Paul is not speaking as the many; there were those who would come in behind him and place the law on the Church, or teach false doctrines in the pursuit of gain. He explains to us that Jesus is the resurrection, He is the life, and we don't need to repay, it has been prepaid. The Kinsman-Redeemer has prevailed and paid our debt; we have been ransomed. He paid our debt at the cross and received our deed through His resurrection. We live in a fellowship with Him because He owns us, and He loves us, oh how He loves us!

Bless the Father, Son, and Holy Ghost for their divine mercy and grace for faith in the finished works of Jesus Christ. Therefore we declare that His mercy is abundant, and His grace can reach all who earnestly call. Tell me therefore how rich am I in Christ: for no gift can be worth more, and no gift has ever cost so much.

CHAPTER ELEVEN

THE SALVATION CODE: 53787

No Other Name

Before we look to the Scriptures I want to point out that we will be looking at only one: the Son of God, Jesus Christ. While it is by the name of Jesus Christ and His completed work that we are saved, He has many names. Therefore we should look at some interesting facts concerning His names in both the Old and New Testament. There are 325 to 375 names for the Son of God that type Him in some amazing manners. We will list a few of His names; it is quite impressive and very enlightening.

They are: Almighty, Alpha and Omega, Ancient of Days, Author of Eternal Salvation, Begotten of the Father, Brazen Serpent, Bridegroom, Bright and Morning Star, Builder, Carpenter, Chief Cornerstone, Christ, Christ Jesus, Christ the Power of God, Creditor, Day Star, Deliverer, Desire of All Nations, Elect, Faithful Witness, Firstborn, First and Last, Gift of God, Golden Altar, Governor, Great Shepherd, God, Head of the Church, Husband, Hope of Glory, I Am, Immortal, Jesus Christ, Jesus Christ Our Savior, Judge of Israel, Just Man, King of Kings, King of the Jews, King of Peace, Kinsman-Redeemer, Light of the World, Lion of the

Tribe of Judah, Living Stone, Lord Jesus Christ, Lord of All, Lord of Lords, Melchisedek, Merchant, Mighty God, Most Holy, Most Mighty, Offspring of David, Passover Lamb, Power of God, Precious Cornerstone, Ransom for All, Redeemer, Rock, Root of David, Salvation, Savior, Son of God, Second Adam, Second Man, Shepherd, Son of the Most High, Spiritual Rock, Stone Rejected, Tree of Life, Tried Stone, True Vine, Way, Well of Living Water, Wisdom, Witness, Wonderful, Word of God, Word of Life, Worthy.

These are but a few of the names of our Lord Jesus Christ, and many of these names are located in this study. As stated before, His visits are as many as His names. Before we move on let's add the Holy Ghost and some of His wonderful names.

They are: Comforter, Holy Spirit, Spirit of Christ, Spirit of Faith, Spirit of Glory, Spirit of Grace, Spirit of Life, and Spirit of the Lord, Spirit of Wisdom, True Testimony, and Witness.

These also are but a few of the names of the Holy Ghost. However some you will not see, hear, or find are spirit of flesh, spirit of the natural, spirit of self-righteousness, or spirit of self-importance.

"Neither is there salvation in any other: for there is none other name under heaven given among men, whereby we must be saved" (Acts 4:12).

"Being justified freely by his grace through the redemption that is in Christ Jesus" (Romans 3:24).

When we start to understand, by the Spirit, the power, wisdom, and direction of Almighty God, we see through the revelation of the Author of eternal security, Jesus Christ, into the living Word of God. The Word of God is alive because Jesus Christ rose from the dead and is alive forevermore.

Now as long as the Author is still living (all three: Father, Son, and Holy Ghost), and the plan is on schedule, and those who want to see can, and those who won't will not, then we see, hear, and understand that it is by our faith. We therefore proclaim: all are in Him who hath heard His voice and believe.

When we rightly divide the Word of truth it always leads us back to the finished works of Jesus Christ. The fact that they are finished works explained in the statement is the reason the name of Jesus Christ is the only name by which we must be saved. The living Word can be so clear; it does not tell us "can be saved" or "might be saved," but rather "must be saved." We have to be saved, for the Word declares we must! All victory is in Him for the Lamb of God hath prevailed!

The work has been done, the dispensation of grace by faith is soon to be at a close, and the throne of grace will move to a throne of judgment for seven years. It is grace by faith: the greatest gift in the world, a gift that we should know our salvation is complete and therefore our resurrection assured, for His name is the Word of Life.

Jesus Christ according to the living Word is the name above all names, praise the Father, the Son, and the Holy Ghost, amen.

Not by Works of the Flesh

"And all flesh died that moved upon the earth, both of fowl, and of cattle, and of beast, and of every creeping thing that creepeth upon the earth, and every man: all in whose nostrils was the breath of life, all that was in the dry land, died" (Genesis 7:21-22).

"And they fell upon their faces, and said, O God, the God of the spirits of all flesh, shall one man sin, and wilt thou be wroth with all the congregation?" (Numbers 16:22).

"For I know that my redeemer liveth and that he shall stand in the latter day upon the earth: and so after my skin worms destroy this body, yet in my flesh shall I see God" (Job 19:25-26).

"And further by these, my son, be admonished: of making many books there is no end; and much study is a weariness of the flesh" (Ecclesiastes 12:12).

"Watch and pray, that you enter not into temptation: the spirit indeed is willing, but the flesh is weak" (Matthew 26:41).

"And the word was made flesh, and dwelt among us, (and we beheld His glory, the glory as the only begotten of the Father,) full of grace and truth"
(John 1:14).

"There is therefore no condemnation to them which are in Christ Jesus, who walk not after the flesh, but after the spirit" (Romans 8:1).

"Keeping yourselves in the love of God, looking for the mercy of our Lord Jesus Christ unto eternal life. And of some have compassion, making a difference: and others save with fear, pulling them out of the fire; hating even the garment spotted by the flesh. Now unto him that is able to keep you from falling, and to present you faultless before the presence of His glory with exceeding joy, to the only wise God our Savior, be glory and majesty, dominion and power, both now and ever. Amen" (Jude 21-25).

The first thing we need to understand is that our flesh dies, and in fact it is seen as already dead. We are all as a dead man walking. All we need to realize this is to look in our family photo albums. It doesn't matter how much wealth we have or don't have, we all start on the road to death from day one. It can be said that no matter when the picture is taken, we are always younger! Death is the payment for missing the mark. While all mankind is already seen as dead by God the Father, the saved are seen as dead and raised. We are accounted as dead through the death of our Lord and accounted as raised by the glorious resurrection of Jesus Christ.

The next thing we hear, when we hear, is the question: will one man's sin affect all of us? To believe and comprehend this all we need to do is watch the news all day for a day or two. We can go on the Internet and read the local paper, whatever, and we will see what Satan through the fall of Adam has done to this world. Let us review another item in the Scripture that passes by most of us: "The God of the spirits of all flesh"; interesting that He does not say God of all flesh isn't it?

But we have faith for Job proclaims to us that even when his flesh is destroyed and decayed, in his flesh he will see God. Job believed in the resurrection and the glorified body. Why? By faith, looking forward, he knew his Kinsman-Redeemer would prevail and overcome the world and be alive forever.

When we study, we should pray and ask the Holy Ghost to speak to us and give us strength, because it is hard on our flesh. The natural man does not understand the things of God. The Word of God, the Son of God, was made flesh, not a visit, but a family member, and this family member was full of grace and truth, and His glory was seen. He therefore contained the relationship, the freedom, the willingness, and the means to pay for our debt, thus providing the requirements of the law to be our Kinsman-Redeemer. He hath redeemed our deed, and He truly loves us. There is one last lesson here: many modernists today teach that Jesus never claimed to be God. Jude, James, Paul, Peter, Luke, John, Mark, and Matthew would dispute that.

As the result of this Redeemer and the events that surrounded His finished works, Paul can declare "there is now no more condemnation" when we put our faith and trust in the things that remain. As with Joshua, neither man nor angel can condemn us.

We are implored to trust God by our faith in the mercy provided through Jesus Christ, in whom we have eternal life. We are told to testify by fear to some and kindness to others, whatever it takes to pull them out of the fire. We must keep our faith in Him for He is the one who keeps us from falling out of His grace. He not only keeps us from falling but presents us as faultless; He didn't say we were faultless but rather presented faultless. We therefore see that the penalty has been paid.

"For I know that in me (that is in my flesh) dwelleth no good thing: for to will is present with me; how to perform that which is good I find not" (Romans 7:18).

We should all know this feeling; the greatest among all apostles, Paul, cannot overcome the flesh. He struggles and fights with his natural man, as we do. In fact Paul says it is a daily battle. His faith is in Jesus Christ and he puts his trust in Him, for His love is great toward us, His mercy forever toward us, and His grace is enough for us. It is through this faith that Paul can proclaim "I have finished the course, I have kept the faith" (2 Timothy 4:7).

He does not claim that he has kept the law, or lived perfectly, but rather kept his faith. He had formed the Church, he had completed his work, and he had stayed his course. Soon they would kill him for the witness of Jesus Christ.

Paul is all but completely alone. At this point almost all have forsaken him, but he has kept his faith. This was the greatest of all earthly born men. Through Paul by Jesus Christ and the power of the Holy Ghost was the truth of the mystery hidden by God revealed and given unto us.

"But we have this treasure in earthen vessels, that the excellency of the power may be of God, and not of us" (2 Corinthians 4:7).

The Just Shall Live by Faith

"Behold his soul which is lifted up is not upright in him: but the just shall live by faith" (Habakkuk 2:4).

"Then Jesus answered and said unto her, O woman, great is thy faith; be it unto thee even as thou wilt. And her daughter was made whole that very hour" (Matthew 15:28).

"And he said to the woman, Thy faith hath saved thee; go in peace" (Luke 7:50).

"And God, which knoweth the hearts, bare them witness, giving them the Holy Ghost, even as he did unto us; and put no difference between us and them, purifying their hearts by faith" (Acts 15:8-9).

"Therefore being justified by faith, we have peace with God through our Lord Jesus Christ: by whom also we have access by faith into this grace wherein we stand, and rejoice in the hope of the glory of God" (Romans 5:1).

"Watch ye, stand fast in the faith, quit you like men, be strong" (1 Corinthians 16:13).

"For by grace are ye saved through faith; and that not of yourselves; it is the gift of God" (Ephesians 2:8).

"Looking unto Jesus the author and finisher of our faith, who for the joy that was set before him endured the cross, despising the shame, and is set down at the right hand of the throne of God" (Hebrews 12:2).

"Who are kept by the power of God through faith unto salvation ready to be revealed in the last time" (1 Peter 1:5).

The living Word of God is both beautiful and powerful to behold. Neither other book nor any collection of writings can span sixteen hundred years always operating in the future, and always correct. With no regard as to the point in time in which it stands, for it always stands as history written in advance. And it shall stay that way until all be fulfilled. The living Word operates with great passion, power, anger, judgment, salvation, redemption, love, and glory as no other, telling of the Kinsman-Redeemer and the finished works of Him: Jesus the Christ.

Forty scribes of one author, and thus we see that the living Word fits together as a perfect building, built by a perfect Builder. Forty men were chosen to write this collection of 66 books and letters. As we have seen the scribes came from a wide range of backgrounds. They wrote over a period of almost 1,600 years with 807,361 words, 31,173 verses, and 1,189 chapters. These 40 men collaborated on the greatest collection of spiritual and historical documents in the world. It is put together like the perfectly built universe, created by a divine Creator.

These great men did not get lucky. Instead, it appears they had inside information. We can see and hear the living Word speak. When "rightly divided" it does not matter where we pull our information. When we are on subject and context the truth in the Word will fit together with perfection. It is a living thing that we hold in our hands, or lay upon our table or desk: to see and to hear that we may better know the love of God.

The living Word must continue to come to pass or it will die! We know this is not possible, for we are told "heaven and earth will pass away, but my words will never pass away."

Concerning faith, we see that it heals and saves and that by it we are justified. If we are then justified, we should be at peace. If we are at peace then by grace, given through the Lord Jesus Christ, it is both the gift and glory of God. We should stand tall. Don't quit. Hang in there. Why? Because by grace we are given victory through faith in the finished works of the Lord Jesus Christ

Having our faith grounded in truth, that He is both Author and Finisher of our faith and that for that faith He endured the cross and the beatings, being spat upon, cursed, and humiliated. Even as He was being nailed to the cross, still He cried out "forgive them, Father, for they know not what they do." Such love hath no man received by any other. He then sat down at the right hand of the Father, upon the throne of grace, and by Him are we held until we are revealed, as His glory in the latter time.

"It is better to trust in the Lord than to put confidence in man" (Psalm 118:8).

The center of the living Word is the centerpiece of all history, the First and Last, Jesus Christ.

"Who is a God like unto thee that pardoneth iniquity and passeth by the transgressions of the remnant of his heritage? He retained not his anger for ever, because he delighteth in mercy" (Micah 7:18).

Before we start block eleven, let us review where we are in the unfolding history within the living Word of God. We are in the present age and under the dispensation of grace by faith. At this time Jesus Christ sits upon the throne of grace, until the fullness of the Gentiles be brought in. At some point soon He will call out a people for His name and He will move to a throne of judgment. Both are just, for He is justified.

We have gone from the flood to the moon, and still not much has changed. Oh, the world is modified, things are remodeled, advancements are made. But we, we don't change much, do we. For almost two thousand years we have been under the throne and government of grace by faith. God has spoken to us by the prophets, and in these last days by His Son.

Jesus Christ has cleaned up the mess started by Adam; He has kept all of His covenants with Israel and with the Church. That which is yet to come has come, for "God sees those things that be not as though they were." Therefore we now know that the future covenants have been kept, "for heaven and earth will pass away, but my words will never pass away."

Our prayer is that we will know from where our salvation comes, why it comes, and from whom it comes.

CHAPTER TWELVE

THE COMING OF THE KING: CODE NAME SAVIOR

In this section we are going to review the future work of Almighty God through the Holy Ghost and the Lord Jesus Christ. We will present hard Scripture to support the claim that there is still work to be done, but that it is done because God declares it. Many within the world of Christian thought claim the Bible has been fulfilled with the exception of the second coming, and others claim there is no rapture. While both of these thoughts are common they are also serious misunderstandings. Let us look at the facts as presented by the living Word concerning the amount of work that Almighty God hath predetermined by decree and therefore shall be completed.

Israel was born again as a nation on May 14, 1948, and therefore the clock of God has started to tick once more and the postponement placed on Israel and the kingdom has come to an end. For almost two thousand years God through Christ and the labor of the Holy Ghost has been at work calling out a people for His name. Lives have been changed and men and women saved through the testimony of the Holy Ghost. People are still healed, and He is gathering His Body and

Bride; soon the Church and Body will be complete. Signs and wonders will once again come to the forefront, "for the Jew requires a sign," and they with many more that are left behind will soon see far too many.

The Future Work

There is so much information here that we must narrow our study. We must take that which we now know and apply it to that which we will see.

"Seventy weeks are determined upon thy people and upon thy holy city, to finish the transgression, to make an end of sins, and to make reconciliation for iniquity, and to bring in everlasting righteousness, and to seal up the vision and prophecy, and to anoint the most Holy" (Daniel 9:24).

This is a 490-year vision, and the vision concerns Daniel's people, the nation of Israel and thus the Jewish people. The 490 years do not run concurrently; there is a gap. The last seven years have been postponed now for over 2,000 years. How do we know this? The living Word shows us that which was to come, and is come, as well as that which is to come and shall come.

We know that the transgression was finished at the cross. We know that Jesus Christ is declared to have defeated sin and overcome the world. He is declared our reconciliation, thus we know that these three events have been completed. But within the same verse we see that three events have not yet come to pass. At this point in history most of us can understand: we have not seen anything that appears like everlasting righteousness upon this earth. As far as anointing the Most Holy, or the crowning Jesus Christ upon the throne of David if you will. I think this one would have made the papers and the news of the day. But nowhere in history, of any period, any nation or empire, has one historian bothered to record what would have been a most historic event. Therefore the vision cannot be sealed and the prophecy is still alive.

We now can see three events that were completed over two thousand years ago and three events yet to be completed. But they are in the same verse. Yes they are; that does not change the fact that we have six items and events foretold and we know by history that only three are complete. In the same manner as with the prophet Isaiah we have a gap located within the Scripture. Daniel was dealing with Israel and simply was not allowed to see the gap concerning the dispensation of grace. Many theologians do the same and fail to see the gulf of time between these six historical events.

Once again this is so similar to the prophet Isaiah and the information we earlier saw concerning the same Most Holy. As with Isaiah, Daniel is also seeing three events that are yet to come. We know this as history written in advance. Thus we have established both by history and the Word of God the gap, and the dispensation of grace. Again we see two truths here with clarity. First, the Church was not seen by Daniel, but the time was allotted for it. And second, contrary to those who teach that the Church has replaced Israel, the Word denies this. For when the Church is caught out we clearly see He will once again turn His thoughts to Israel.

Let us understand Israel must be in power as a nation for the prophecy clock of God to operate; we've been in a long time-out during the dispensation of grace by faith. As stated the clock started again on May 14, 1948. We by this understanding can now see at some point in the near future the events of the prophecy yet to be fulfilled, but as with the others they too shall soon come to pass.

In recent months we have seen an ever increasing destabilizing of almost all the Middle East Muslim counties, and the ever increasing pressure on Israel to give up ground. When we see these events take place then things should come to mind for the Church as well as Israel, for the rapture event is now on the clock if you will. The rapture is the next big historical event.

"For the Lord himself shall descend from heaven with a shout, with the voice of the archangel, and the trump of God: and the dead in Christ will rise first: then we which are alive and remain shall be caught up together with them in the clouds, to meet the Lord in the air: and so shall we forever be with the Lord. Wherefore comfort one another with these words" (1 Thessalonians 4:16-18).

"For God hath not appointed us to wrath, but to obtain salvation by our Lord Jesus Christ, who died for us, that, whether we wake or sleep, we should live together with Him" (1 Thessalonians 5:9-10).

I would put the rapture or catching away as the next major event in the future work of the Trinity: the Father, Son, and Holy Ghost. Something tells us that this is a pretty big event, and as we will see it is and has remained a mysterious event.

Paul is extremely clear; here he uses the term salvation rather than redemption. Why? We need to remember that salvation is deliverance from destruction. This should be an easy one for us to read between the lines. It will be with a shout, but only the blood-washed believers will hear it, for it is the trump of God to call the people throughout the land. It will be the voice of the archangel of God. We are told that the dead and the living are taken in order. It is hidden in the clouds; it is not a public event, it is secret, and hath been hidden from the beginning. We will forever be with the Bright and Morning Star, the Lord Jesus Christ, and then it shall be a secret no more.

We are to comfort each other. Just a minute, if there is no rapture why would it be comforting to look forward to the great tribulation? Be not confused, the living Word hath prevailed to show us the truth: we have not been appointed unto wrath but unto salvation by Jesus Christ. It won't matter if we are alive or dead. He will come, He will call, and we will be with Him in the air.

The next major event in world history is the Antichrist and "the time of Jacob's trouble." There is no other subject more debated than this period of time. Men and women wonder: has it happened? Is the book just code for their day? There is no rapture, the Church must be punished, it all ended in 70 AD, it's too much for me, it doesn't concern me. Oh, they've said He would come back forever. What is the truth?

We already know there are people who don't see or hear, and won't see or hear. We know from Daniel and Isaiah that there are prophecies and history still to come, and yet there are many Bible answer men and preachers who want us to believe it was all fulfilled by Titus in 70 AD.

That is somewhat confusing. John is clearly told to write those things which were, which are, and which are to come. John wrote the Revelation twenty to twenty-five years after the Temple was destroyed. Many would have us believe it was all fulfilled at that time in history. Why then is John told to write about past, present, and future? The other problem is 70 AD went right on by and as we have seen they forgot to anoint the Most Holy, and that everlasting thing, that was just a symbolic message. If this were true then the book has died and the vision and prophecy have been completed and God's Word is not true. This as we have seen is not the truth.

The books of Daniel and Revelation are not symbolic books. What they are is history written in advance. That a symbolic writing style is used does not alter the fact that these events are predetermined to take place and were designed to come to light in the latter days. Just as the ancient witness, the Great Pyramid, is to be understood in that day. As with the parables some will see and hear and believe and some will not. The Holy Ghost has always been writing the future, always! After 2,555 years Israel is a nation again; we can stake it all on that one fact. So what is the truth?

"And he shall confirm the covenant with many for one week and in the midst of the week he shall cause the sacrifice and the oblation to cease, and for the overspreading of abominations he shall make it desolate, even until the consummation, and that determined shall be poured upon the desolate" (Daniel 9:27).

Daniel is being told the things which are to come concerning his people. This is the one coming in his own name, the little horn, Antichrist, that they will believe him. Having failed to believe Jesus Christ when He came in His Father's name, they rejected Him the first time: they did not know their King.

They will now follow a false shepherd, a fake. The nation of Israel was not in power in 70 AD, and they did not nor have they accepted a king to this day. Therefore we can rest assured that this is yet to come. The counterfeit christ will sign a peace treaty with Israel to provide safety, or the slogan of the day, "peace and security." After three and a half years he will break the covenant with them and enter the temple, declare himself god, and sacrifice an unclean animal. The temple, because of his actions, is desolate once again. That is until the King of Kings and Lord of Lords returns and lays claim to the promised throne of David.

We can know that this is history written in advance by the living Word of God, for all the world wants peace in the Middle East and it all revolves around the tiny nation of Israel. We can already see that the new Egyptair map has removed Israel, and as other nations fall this kind of thing will continue

At this time many are betting that Israel will hit Iran in an attempt to stop the nuclear threat near its borders. And in fact by the time you read this it could have happened. We already hear the cry of peace and security ringing out as the world cries peace, peace, peace, and all the while governments are embroiled in war. It is through examples such as these that we as believers and those in the secular world know a treaty of some kind must come.

However at this point no such treaty has ever been recorded in history. To this account, and to this fact, we can again conclude that these events are yet to be fulfilled. But they are complete in the mind of God for the Ancient of Days hath spoken.

"After this I looked and a door was opened in heaven: and the first voice that I heard was as it were of a trumpet talking with me; who said come up hither, and I will shew thee things which must be hereafter" (Revelation 4:1).

"And I saw in the right hand of him that sat on the throne a book written within and on the backside sealed with seven seals" (Revelation 5:1).

Once again the words are from the Lord Jesus Christ, to John, as a type of the Church. He is taken up before the events he is to see unfold: "the time of Jacob's trouble," Daniel's seventieth week, the great tribulation!

He sees the deed to the earth sealed with seven seals. We must understand that the deed was taken from Adam in the garden, and after the cross it was taken by the Lord Jesus Christ and placed in escrow, waiting for a closing date; the fullness of the Gentiles being brought in is the closing date.

No one can close on the transaction until the Lamb of God, Jesus Christ, steps up and prevails to complete the transaction. Notice this: no one who is already there is worthy of handling this transaction and it broke John's heart. Jesus is worthy for the throne of grace must become a throne of judgment. While this transformation is prepared the Church grows, it waits as we say "for everyman." As we have seen this is until the fullness of the Gentiles be brought in, waiting on that last man, woman, or child to accept the testimony of the Holy Ghost.

That the deed is perfect we see through the seven seals. It is this transaction that requires a just and perfect Redeemer to redeem a just and perfect deed. There will be seven seals, seven trumpets, and seven bowls or vials. These are judgments upon Israel, upon false worship, no worship, and a world that has rejected the throne of grace by faith.

The Church, Body, and Bride are men and women from every nation and tongue, and who have been caught out. The great and terrible day of His wrath hath come. Almighty God will judge Israel and the godless men who have followed the false christ and his false prophet.

There are many amazing events in the book of Daniel and its continuation by John: the Revelation of Jesus Christ. It will be a time of great tribulation as never has been and never will be again. The judgments are of all kinds, earthquakes, pestilence, hunger, stars falling, the sun darkened, the moon as blood, mountains falling into the seas, rivers turning blood red and drying up. And Antichrist will rule the world with a one-world government, church, and economic system. It is a time of famine, disease, and warfare both supernaturally and earthly and many will die; no words can explain this save the Word of God.

We can see every day how the world gets smaller, and we hear the call for a New World Order. Soon, very soon, if not already the world will be able through computers to speak one language and all will hear. We watch as radical governmental changes take place throughout the Middle East. We can now start to see the false church. As we watch the many false teachers tell us we must be tolerant, we must work together, we see the start of "Chrislam" and the Koran placed in pews of false churches. While these false and unholy teachers and leaders claim to know Christ, they may know of Him but they do not know Him.

At the middle of the week, about the time Antichrist enters the temple, Almighty God will send forth two witnesses; according to most theologians they will be either Enoch and Elijah or Moses and Elijah. According to the Word there should be little debate. The Word is clear on this for the prophets Enoch and Elijah share one unique quality: neither has died. "It is appointed once for men to die then the judgment" (Hebrews 9:27). We can clearly see that up to this point they have missed that event.

They will preach in the city of Jerusalem for three and a half years, performing great and wondrous works in the name of the Almighty. They will call out the judgments upon the earth and the people of earth will hate them. They shall be killed, their bodies left on the street, and the people of the earth will rejoice at their death. But after three days they will rise again, and this will signal that the end of this seven-year period of judgment is about complete. This is the wrath of God, and save for His mercy and that the days be cut short, there would be no flesh living.

"The LORD is a man of war: the LORD is His name" (Exodus 15:3).

"And the armies that were in heaven followed him upon white horses, clothed in fine linen, white and clean. And out of his mouth goeth a sharp sword, that with it he should smite the nations: and he shall rule them with a rod of iron:

and he treadeth the winepress of the fierceness and the wrath of almighty God" (Revelation 19:14-15).

"And he laid hold on the dragon, that old serpent, which is the devil, and Satan, and bound him, a thousand years" (Revelation 20:2).

So much for the pacifist Jesus; He hath already turned the other cheek! It seems we are all guilty of forgetting which Kinsman is coming. Is it the one before the cross or the one who has risen? Is it thorns upon His head or a golden crown? Upon His thigh is it written "Lamb of God, Shepherd" or "King of Kings and Lord of Lords"? Is it now that the prophet be right: the Lord is a man of war? Our Lord now has hair as wool, His face is radiant, His eyes are as coals of fire, He wears a golden girdle, He wears the crown of a king, and His feet are as polished brass. He is the glorified Lord, no more beatings, no more cross to bear—those events have been completed. The glorified Lord is a man of war and He treads the winepress of the wrath of God. Today He is the Most Mighty, the Bright and Morning Star, the Faithful and True, and in righteousness doth He judge and make war (Revelation 19:11).

The earth is going through the great tribulation, Israel finally sees her mistake, out of her twelve tribes come 144,000 preachers, sealed in the forehead and protected by God. They will once again, as in the days of old, preach the gospel to the ends of the earth that the kingdom of heaven is at hand. This great testimony, that the true witness will for one last time reach out to man, will indeed save many souls, but sadly not enough.

Most humans left on the earth will be killed. All will turn against Israel; they will blame the Jews and make way to come against her and destroy her, but the Lord Jesus Christ returns and saves her at His second coming, seven years after the rapture. This is the revelation of Jesus Christ. Satan is locked up for one thousand years, and peace will be upon the earth.

"And when the thousand years were expired, Satan shall be loosed out of his prison. And shall go out to deceive the nations which are in the four quarters of the earth, Gog and Magog, to gather them together for battle: the number of whom is as the sand of the sea. And they went up on the breadth of the earth, and compassed the camp of the saints about, and the beloved city. And fire came down from God out of heaven and devoured them. And the devil that had deceived them was cast into the lake of fire and brimstone, where the beast and false prophet are, and shall be tormented day and night forever and ever" (Revelation 20:7-10).

"And I John saw the holy city New Jerusalem coming down from God out of heaven, prepared as a bride adorned for her husband" (Revelation 21:2).

    The people of the earth will live as did Adam and Eve for years and years, all while under the rule of a peaceful and prosperous King and royal people. Israel will fulfill her role as a leader of nations in civil matters, legal matters, and worship. As to the Church, we have been caught out at the beginning of the week. Remember Rebekah when she jumped off the camel? Was she not already adorned and did not Isaac go to meet her?
    The Lord is on the throne; the lion and the calf, the wolf and the lamb eat and sleep together. There is no war, no hunger, and no Satan, for he is locked up with his followers; the tempter hath been removed. And they all lived happily ever... Not quite.
    When Satan is let out he will find willing men again, Nimrods who wish to overthrow the Most High. Satan will

come with an army numbering as the sand. Satan with his army of many will be from all over the world. They encompass and surround the City of God to make war with the Lamb. The Father will send fire out of heaven and destroy them. Satan is cast into the lake of fire forever.

Many scholars and personalities today believe this to be the war before Christ assumes the throne of David. Many teachers claim this happens at Armageddon at the end of the seven-year great tribulation. Why on earth this is debated should be a mystery to us. This is clearly what Ezekiel was foretelling in chapters 38 and 39. There are several easy clues. First, they are living in unprotected cities, and they will not let their defenses down under a seven-year treaty. Second, Satan has been bound a thousand years, and the Kinsman Jesus Christ is operating as a King, a High Priest, and a Messiah. He is not ruling as the Father, but rather in the Father's name, just as when He came the first time. On His thigh is not written Everlasting Father or God of Gods, but rather King of Kings and Lord of Lords. This time the Father, showing power and great glory, puts down the rebellion, the last rebellion.

Then in the fullness of time Christ the High Priest will purify the heaven and earth with fire and present His finished works to the Father. The Father will join the Son and Holy Ghost. The world which has seen a King will now behold the glory of heaven by the Father. The glory that we have been seeing the world will see. Then the New Jerusalem shall descend from heaven. The pure river of life is opened and earth and heaven have been renovated. The Father comes to reside and the perfect age, eternity—the ages of the ages—begins. We must learn to rightly divide the Word of truth. It is sometimes easier to see when it is divided correctly.

"And I heard a great voice out of heaven saying; Behold, the tabernacle of God is with men and he will dwell with them and they shall be his people and God himself will be with them; and be their God" (Revelation 21:3).

Let us ask one question. Does it mean what it says? If it does, then this is the first time God the Father is going to live with man. We know both by secular as well as biblical history that Jesus has already lived with mankind. We know by history written in advance that in fact He will be living with man for one thousand years. It is also promised to us the indwelling of the Holy Ghost, so He also has lived here. So it becomes clear as to when these events take place, who is already here, and who is coming, as in guess who's providing salvation this time? He's the Father and He's coming to the feast.

"I Jesus have sent my angel to testify unto you these things in the churches. I am the root and offspring of David, and the bright and morning star" (Revelation 22:16).

The Almighty God hath put His truth in a living Word that we might know of Him and His unequaled love for us. God wants no flesh to perish and has repeatedly provided man with proof of Himself and His power, wisdom, and direction. His love is never ending, His mercy is longsuffering, His grace is forever, and His reward is eternal.

Throughout history man has seen fit to turn away from God, to turn to false gods, to deny that which can be seen, and to ignore that which can be heard. Each has turned to his own way and that is the way of Cain.

Sin has affected everything that we see and touch. The stain of sin has no cleaner save the blood of the Lamb: Jesus Christ. For we have all sinned and fallen short of the perfect glory of God. In fact sin has corrupted the whole creation as we are told it groans for the day of deliverance. We are all in need of an Advocate with the Father, one who will pay the price of our debt, one who will willingly redeem us from the fate we are due. We need a Faithful and True Kinsman-Redeemer, we need Jesus Christ.

His judgment is just and His verdict is final. There are no appeals, there are no higher courts. Man decides upon heaven or hell by his own heart. God, as the Judge, only pronounces the sentence. Let's be honest; it's not like we haven't been told how the transaction works.

We hold the power of choosing everlasting life and joy...or everlasting death and torment. It is in our mouth and in our heart. The power to confess ourselves to salvation is in our power, to call upon the Kinsman-Redeemer, Jesus Christ, put faith in His finished works, and receive the free gift of grace, God's divine mercy. By the witness of the Holy Ghost, He knocks on each door daily. We are our own jury, God is the Judge, and we are all guilty, for all have missed the mark. The question becomes how do we arrange the pardon? Maybe with the offer that is already on the table.

CHAPTER THRITEEN

THERE IS NONE LIKE ME: CODE NAME ALPHA

Within the pages of the Bible is contained the living Word of God. If we are to go by who it says we are it becomes clear that we need a Savior. The time is short. When looking at this planet and where it is, and who is in charge, we wonder how and when it all should end. Where is hope and where oh where is sanity? It is not in government, and it is hard to find in far too many churches. All we need to do is watch the news, read a paper, or go online to see the depravity of mankind. We can find it everywhere and it is not uplifting. Government debts are everywhere and in every nation and owed to who? Who are these few? Who is their god?

There Can Be Only One: Code Name I AM

We can feel the wind blow, we can hear the thunder, and we can see the lightning. And we know there is a storm coming. We can feel the hate against His name, we can see the result, and we can hear the false teaching. We know there is a falling away.

We can hear the cries of the hungry, we can see the starvation, and we can feel the greed. We sell corn and wheat for fuel while people starve. There is a New World Order coming. We can feel the revolt of the earth, we can see the devastation, and we can hear the rumblings. The birth pains have begun.

We can hear when summer is coming, for the sounds are in the air. We can feel fall give way to winter with the chill in the air. We can see spring as the fig tree blooms. There is a rapture coming.

We have heard it all before and it never changes, it has always worked. That old serpent, the devil, has stuck to his plan; be like God, be your own god, anything you want, love this world, just like Lot's wife. How is it we fail to see that which we were told of, for the Word doth declare it will all come to pass.

"In my Father's house are many mansions; if it were not so, I would have told you. I go to prepare a place for you, and if I go and prepare a place for you, I will come again, and receive you unto myself; that where I am, there you may be also" (John 14: 2-3).

For the believer we can come to know Him in a more faithful way, we can come to trust His love, we can come to see His grace, and we can come to hear His living Word and realize true joy. The Faithful and True Witness has already come, and He is about to return.

Jesus Christ is the only truth there is. For all this world has to offer is contrary to the truth of God. The living Word will speak to us when we aspire to call upon God.

"Call upon me and I will answer thee, and shew thee great and mighty things, that thou knowest not" (Jeremiah 33:3).

God's phone number is provided to all through the living Word of God. That He is there and will answer is promised. For He says call and I will answer. That the world will seek that of itself is evident in the false worship of dead men and the religions that proudly proclaim Him still on the cross. There are churches that misuse the living Word and deny the power thereof. The evangelist whose love is for the riches of this world and promotes the Lord God as a pimp, to provide our every wish—he is accursed.

To those who tell us that He is the brother who has shown us the way, that we can be as gods—doesn't it all sound like the garden all over again? Let us pray for the many denominations that do not preach on the saving power of the cross, of the blood, and of the resurrection of Jesus Christ. For this is the only power unto salvation. To those whose wisdom is of the natural and not the spirit, and who will not see the two creations and do not rightly divide the Word, pray for them for they are living within their own enlightenment and limit the rules and power of Almighty God.

But mighty is the Lord of Hosts, and mighty is He indeed! He hath prevailed to bring us redemption, salvation, righteousness, and glory that by His hand we are delivered out of the world unto the resurrection of the just. That we who have been hidden in Him by the power of God from the beginning, for the sake of His Son, our Savior Jesus Christ, can be where He is also.

That by His will we are justified and by His finished works we are given wisdom and direction to overcome this world. He has given us the gift of eternal life by His unequaled love. Such love and joy we will never equal, nor can the natural man comprehend.

As to the non-believer we can pray for their salvation and hope we have provided insight into the power that is unto salvation through the living Word of God. That he who is lost shall be found. To the one who is blind that he shall see, and to the one who is deaf that he should hear. To those throughout the world who live in darkness that the Light of the World would shine. To the false religions and false teachers of the day, we are instructed by Paul through the wisdom of the Holy Ghost:

"As we have said before, so say I now again, if any man preach any other gospel unto you than that ye have received, let him be accursed" (Galatians 1:9).

"But I certify you, brethren, that the gospel that was preached of me is not after man. For I neither received it of man, neither was I taught it, but by the revelation of Jesus Christ" (Galatians 1:11-12).

Paul wants us to know that from that point on it is his gospel; this is the gospel whereby we are saved and mankind is judged. It is by his revelation, not given by man, but through Jesus Christ, that the mystery of grace through faith hath been revealed, that the secret from the beginning is revealed through Paul by Jesus Christ in us.

We can clearly see that the Word of God is a living thing, and the living Word of God is Jesus Christ. That Jesus Christ is the True Witness of God the Father. That all things are in Christ and Christ is in the Father. Therefore if we be in Christ and Christ in us, then are we not already in the Father? Praise be to God.

"And hath raised us up together, and made us sit together in heavenly places in Christ Jesus" (Ephesians 2:6).

Paul uses the word *hath*, a past event that has already been completed; therefore if we be in the Father through the Son, will not the Father keep the entire treasure that was hid in the field? Was it not purchased by the blood of His Son?

That we should lay hold of and have eternal security, for does not the living Word of God say that He hath raised us up, and if raised up, is not Christ seated, and are we not in Christ, yea, seated on the right hand?

"Now to Him that is of power to stablish you according to my gospel, and the preaching of Jesus Christ, according to the revelation of the mystery, which was kept secret since the world began" (Romans 16:25).

"Remember the former things of old: I Am God, and there is none else; I Am God, and there is none like me" (Isaiah 46:9).

To God the Father, to the Son, and to the Holy Ghost be glory forever and ever. Amen.

Does Anybody Really Know What Time It Is?

I have stated that I endorse no single denomination, for our salvation is in the power of God not in denominations. However we are free to select our own church and our own belief, though it should be based on the Word of God, so discern well, beloved. While there are men and women of God in all Christian denominations and in every nation of the world, we must be always discerning and put our trust in God.

Where each believer and non-believer attends church is the right of each individual. Many preachers and teachers are still teaching, or attempting to teach, "the rightly divided Word." May the Lord Jesus Christ bless each and every one of them.

In the United States we are currently free to have our head so far up our backside that we can't see. There seems to be more watered down and false teaching in the world today than truth teaching: the saving power of God by the finished works of Jesus Christ, this is the truth.

The people of the United States are currently free to be of any denomination they wish; there are hundreds of them from A to Z. We can trust in Jesus Christ, the Kinsman-Redeemer, or we can believe something short of that. We can even make believe we are a god, kind of like a little god. We can believe in a higher power, in ourselves, and even spacemen or false gods. Why, we can even make believe there is no God. God has given us those rights; it is not by force but rather by faith or lack thereof that no man can stand blameless before the throne of judgment.

But there are countries where we cannot be free to worship. Places where if we are caught with the Bible we can be killed. Places where if we speak His name we could be killed. If we don't believe as they do we might be killed. In these countries it is the law and religion, there is no such thing as separation of church and state. Meanwhile in those countries there are believers whose lives are on the line every single day. Their faith I commend and do marvel at. May God bless each of them. Amen.

This is a sinful world we live in, and the prince of this age and this world has done all he can to destroy the living Word of God, but it is still alive. And it is not alone in bearing witness to its truth, for just men and women throughout history have given their lives for the truth of this living Word.

It does not bear witness to dead things or dead men, but rather to the living. It does not bear witness to strapping bombs to our children, or to being "the brother who showed us the way." It does not speak of us becoming a god; it does not elevate any man, woman, or other save the Lord Jesus Christ. It will not tell us He is in all of us, for He is not. The fact that He wants to be in all does not alter the fact that He is not. He will not force Himself into our hearts.

We should always be mindful of the wonderful painting of Him knocking at the door. It is speaking to us, revealing His great love for us, for there is no door handle on the outside; He must be invited in. We should realize He respects our rights; after all He gave them to us! It does not bear witness to us dying for Him, but rather Him dying for us. Don't believe they are the same; it cannot be more different, it cannot be reconciled.

Still by and large the world will have none of it. There are those among us who are trying to remove His name from all things government and make the Creator's name an offense. The world will tolerate false gods and unjust men, but do not speak the name of Jesus Christ. The Faithful and True Witness is the only name by which we must be saved. Well, beloved, these men and women too will stand before Him, and they too will confess before they are discarded to the lake of fire "that Jesus Christ is Lord."

He is still knocking and not just for us to be saved, but to be with us, to speak with us, and to help us understand the gravity of our future and what it means to receive the new wine of the True Vine. By giving us the truth we see what it also means to those who reject the truth. May we pull some of them out of the fire by love or by fear; let's just pull some out.

"For what does it profit a man to gain the world and lose his soul?" (Mark 8:46).

He was perfect, He is perfect, and He always will be perfect. That we can be with Him outside of that: was not possible. So He made a way for us to "receive perfection" so that those who will believe...shall be...where He is also.

"And I will pray the Father, and he shall give another Comforter, that he may abide with you forever. Even the

Spirit of truth: Whom the world cannot receive, because it seeth him not, neither knoweth him; but ye know him; for he dwelleth with you and in you" (John 14:16-17).

"Now the God of peace that brought again from the dead our Lord Jesus, that great Shepherd of the sheep, through the blood of the everlasting covenant, make you perfect in every good work to do his will, working in you that which is well pleasing in his sight, through Jesus Christ; to whom be glory forever and ever. Amen" (Hebrews 13:20-21).

    The great Creator will pray on our behalf and the Father will send another Comforter. For you see He is not only the Kinsman, the Savior, the Power and all the others, but a Comforter also. The Father will now send the Holy Ghost forth. Not just to witness, not only to testify and declare, but now to henceforth be in us. Providing us with wisdom to discern, to witness, to testify and declare. He is no longer a visitor but rather a resident.

    We can now therefore declare these truths: the Father and the Son and the Holy Ghost "is one." That the living Word of God is a living Word. That He hath sent His Comforter unto us, to be with us and in us. That He is with us always, even unto the end of the age. That He is not received by the world. That He cannot be seen of the world. That He is not even known in the world. That He is God and there is none other. That the Father hath raised Him from the dead. That He is our Great Shepherd, our Kinsman-Redeemer. That by His blood is the covenant everlasting. That forever Thy Word is settled in heaven.

    We therefore proclaim by the living Word of God: "once we are saved we are redeemed and if redeemed then delivered and if delivered then forever.

    For it is the will of God, unto salvation. That it is by the power given the Tried Stone Jesus Christ; that the natural man who is of the world cannot understand. Therefore he cannot know, and if he cannot know then he cannot receive. That He, rather by the Holy Spirit unto our spirit, that we should know the power of God through Jesus Christ. These were the secret and hidden truths of the everlasting love of Almighty God toward us. These truths proclaim His love from the beginning that all might be given a way to Him, and by the living Word of God "all men have heard the Word."

We within the dispensation of grace by faith are more blessed than all before us, for we are subject to the throne of grace. That at the time of our judgment we may present the finished works of Jesus Christ unto the Father and our faith thereof. Be as the Great Pyramid and build us therefore on the Solid Rock and not the sand of this world, "putting strength in the things which remain," that when the floods of life come we may stand on dry ground, and when the end comes it may be on resurrection ground.

CHAPTER FOURTEEN

IN THESE LAST DAYS: CODE NAME OMEGA

Are We Before or After? Code Name the Cross

As I have stated there are many anointed ministers, pastors, and teachers in the world today. However, again it is sad that there seem to be more all the time who teach false doctrines. We can be gods, Adam was a god, Jesus was rich, and the kingdom was never offered to the Jew. Get your best life now, buy your holy water, and sow that seed. Come get healed and don't forget the check. Most of these are either conmen or working for the one who wants to give it to us now, that old serpent. Is not the message still the same? Do not they twist the Scriptures for gain?

Some will come as lambs in sheep's clothing but they are ravenous wolves. Be ever mindful of this: when the glory is taken from the Creator who sits upon the throne and is given to the creature. When the creature is given glory and all glory is of the Creator. How then do we the creature seek glory? For who are we that we should command God? It is He that counsels Himself. We can only seek glory in Jesus Christ. For it is He that hath overcome sin, death, hell, and the grave. It is He who has won the victory. And to the victor go the spoils, the Body, the Bride, and the Church. We are the spoils of war. For our Lord is a man of war.

"For whatsoever is born of God overcometh the world: and this is the victory that overcometh the world, even our faith. Who is he that overcometh the world, but he that believeth Jesus is the Son of God" (1 John 5:5-6).

"I thank God through Jesus Christ our Lord. So then with my mind I myself serve the law of God, but with the flesh the law of sin" (Romans 7:25).

"He that hath the Son hath life; and he that hath not the Son of God hath not life" (1 John 5:12).

"In hope of eternal life, which God, that cannot lie, promised before the world began" (Titus 1:2).

What shall be said to these things, are we born of flesh or of God: first of flesh to man and second of spirit unto God. Therefore is it of flesh or of spirit that we overcome? All that was and is to be performed is in Jesus Christ. It was not for our earthly pleasure or our earthly desires, but rather that it was performed for our redemption from sin unto the glory of God. Therefore God, who cannot lie, hath promised even before the world that those who love His appearing may be with Him forever and ever.

We should be ever mindful as to which side of the cross we stand. We were never on the other side of the cross. It certainly seems that most of the churches today are still preaching on the other side of the cross. That's the wrong side. He hath risen, He is the Bright and Morning Star, He is a Mighty Warrior, and He is a man of war.

Jesus Christ: Code Name the Only Name

I make no claim to receiving any new revelation of God, for there is no new revelation of God: only understanding or misunderstanding, only truth or fraud, "for there is no new thing under the sun." What is revealed in the living Word is available to everyone. It is not private. By the living Word of God through Jesus Christ, and by the witness of the Holy Ghost, we can understand.

"But in these last days he hath spoken to us by his Son, whom he appointed heir of all things, and through whom he made the universe" (Hebrews 1:2).

I make no claim to being a prophet of God, for the living Word is the prophet of God. What are we going to hear, tell me what we shall see that is not already with us? For once again the living Word of God declares "there is nothing new under the sun."

I make no claim to being a Bible answer man; this author is still a student. I make no claim that this is the only doctrine, or that there is no other way to heaven. The Son of God, the Kinsman-Redeemer Jesus Christ, makes that statement on His Father's behalf and in His own name. I have chosen to believe the Word of God. For Jesus Christ did speak to all. The Word of the Lord spoke:

"For no man cometh to the Father but by me" (John 14:6).

Therefore we declare: "that by no other name whereby we must be saved."

CODE NAME THE KINSMAN
JESUS CHRIST

Therefore there is no other name given to men whereby we must be saved. We as believers feel pain and sorrow for all who are led astray, and many are in darkness these days. We did not make it so, but the Almighty hath spoken and He hath laid down the rules, the ordnances, and the law. He hath provided untold truth and witness unto every man and woman that we should seek a Savior. His living Word has been provided to us and to all who seek truth. He hath seen fit to disclose His truth, His secrets, and His mysteries within the living Book available to all. You may choose not to believe but the truth of the Word of God cannot be denied.

Therefore no man or woman can stand before Him with excuse, for by the Word all have heard the Word. God hath laid the foundation and built the house; He hath provided Himself the sacrifice. Our Kinsman-Redeemer has closed the transaction. He has done all the work and He paid the full price.

Therefore we should realize He also sets the terms of the agreement and His terms are simple: have faith in His Son, Jesus Christ, and His finished works. As they say it's our gift. We can take it or leave it. May God bless the Church. Amen.

References and Credits

The teaching of: the Holy Ghost.
The living Word of God: the Bible
The sermons of Pastor Bill A. Lindsey
The sermons and website of Pastor Velma Aston
The sermons of Dr. Gene Scott
The radio ministry of Dr. J. Vernon McGee
The website of Frank Dimor
The TV ministry of Les Feldick
The Great Pyramid Decoded by E. Raymond Capt

The works of the late Rev. Clarence Larkin:
Dispensational Truth
Rightly Dividing the Word
The Spirit World
The Book of Revelation
The Book of Daniel

CPSIA information can be obtained at www.ICGtesting.com
Printed in the USA
LVOW130857140512
281624LV00003B/4/P